No Sacred Oxen

In this unorthodox autobiographical collection of essays the reader is invited into a world of travel, teaching, education, entertainment, chess, childhood, adolescence, adulthood, despair, political intrigue, faith and Catholicism. The author, a teacher of English living and working abroad, writes about experiences past and present. What he observes around him resonates with some, while challenging the preconceptions of others.

By the same Author –

A Blogger's Route To A Saner World

No Sacred Oxen

Gary Ross

Arena Books

First published in 2014 by Arena Books

Arena Books
6 Southgate Green
Bury St. Edmunds
IP33 2BL

www.arenabooks.co.uk

Distributed in America by Ingram International, One Ingram Blvd., PO Box
3006, La Vergne, TN 37086-1985, USA.

Gary Ross

No Sacred Oxen

British Library cataloguing in Publication Data. A Catalogue record for this
book is available from the British Library.

ISBN-13   978-1-909421-41-7

BIC classifications:-   BGFA, BGL, HPQ, HPS, HRA.

Printed and bound by Lightning Source UK

Cover design
By Jason Anscomb

Typeset in
Times New Roma

Dedication

For Ayram without whom this book would not have been written.

Contents

Introduction   page -   5

Camino Rebirth   9

The Coach Trip   13

Mud Bunging   18

Like an Eagle in Oman   21

There was a ship   22

What is the difference?   28

Auf dem weg nach Berlin   31

An ode to sadness: Keats   36

Wolf-like peregrinations   39

Incarcerated on Mars   42

What Churchill's early life means to me   45

Swings & Roundabouts   49

The Blue Lorry   53

A day trip to Muscat   54

Answers on a postcard   58

Chow Mein   59

The Venerable Bede   67

Voyage & Return   70

NO SACRED OXEN

Following a Rock Band	page -	73
Window Shopping		77
Secular Myths		78
Stop the cavalry		80
Divine Conscience		83
A letter to those who support the EU		86
The Najdorf		88
Peace in our time		99
Democracy Matters		101
Constantinople		104
Picking Daises with Darwin		107
A concept of God		110
The Life Diving Championship: a leap of Faith		111
No Sacred Oxen		116
Chess themes		117
Freedom		121
The Miner's son		122
Glossary of terms		137
Afterword		140
Epilogue: A night out in Oxford		141

Introduction

In writing this book I hope to have gained an audience otherwise what is the point of writing? But I have also gained some insight into what doesn't make me tick. By reading the poetry of John Milton - how odd that he should go blind and Beethoven deaf - I realized that despair is a prayer to a dark power and that faith is the antidote. Like many others I have tried various ways of overcoming or negating the effects of despair but nothing seemed to work. Too much alcohol nourished despair rather than limit its effect and this illusion has caused much misery in life. So it is good news to find in the words of a 17th century poet an awareness of my condition and confirmation of an effective remedy. From hereon in illusions will be treated with the contempt they deserve but I am not about to go teetotal either. One must be very careful in life to avoid the pitfalls awaiting most of us unless we are either extremely fortunate or wise. But in this experience there are also many happy times and I hope this is apparent in this reading.

I have chosen to write about my life which has been all the more eventful as I see it for teaching abroad and working in countries I would probably not have visited otherwise. Certainly this is true of Saudi Arabia since few tourists are allowed to visit this part of the Middle East. But I also doubt whether I would have visited Oman had teaching not drawn me there for several years. My initial time working abroad, however, was in China where I lived for at least three years and has provided some lasting memories. Unlike the blogs in *A Blogger's Route To a Saner World* the recollections here are often deeper and longer and as a result resonate more truly with my life experience. And this provides further insight into not only teaching abroad but decisions made venturing from childhood to adolescence and into adulthood.

Some of my favourite recollections begin this book such as; *Camino Re-birth*, *The Coach Trip* and, *Mud Bunging*, but there are many others I hope the reader will find of interest.

Martin Luther is chosen as a main subject for discussion in much the same way as Darwin was in the previous book. This time, however, the subject necessarily includes some knowledge on theology and the period known as the Reformation - but it is equally accurate in my view to speak of *The Rebellion*. This medieval story is considered pertinent for it is argued that the roots of our culture and society today have, like ourselves, been shaped by events in the past. All is unveiled in an essay entitled, *The Miner's son*.

My interest in theology stems from when I gave up a career in the civil service aged thirty-three to become a mature student at a theological college in Oxford finally gaining a Bth (hons) Oxon. Of all my educational experiences in life this was the richest and afforded a lifestyle that while frugal was packed with insight and opportunity. It was during this time that I first became aware of how important context is to understanding. For all my previous years working in the civil service this thought had never occurred to me. Yet hardly anything has been written of this time. Perhaps I was too content; studying theology, talking philosophy, playing football, and being in Oxford. So there we have it. This book is a collection of autobiographical adventures with opinions.

Instead of paying for psychotherapy I would advise writing a book instead. Write an autobiography and write until there is nothing more to say. At some point there is likely to be a memory of an occasion when you could have turned right instead of left or said no instead of yes. And on one of these occasions there might be a moment for profound reflection.

This happened while writing, **No Sacred Oxen,** or, more specifically, *There was a ship.* I was made deeply aware that life could have been very different from the way it turned out as recollected in the autobiographical essays in this book. The depth of feeling was such that after writing *There was a ship* I did not eat for three days. This was a *fast* I had never expected but it provided some insight into how things came to be and reasons therein. Nevertheless, and with an ensuing proviso, the grit in the oyster can and does make a pearl. Without this collection of unusual and sometimes life-affirming experiences there would be little for me to write about except family life and who wants to write or read about that?

In *Camino Rebirth* and *Wolf-like Peregrinations* readers will find more reminiscences on a walk across Spain undertaken in the summer of 2004, which took thirty-two days to complete. For some this means walking five to ten hours a day from the foot of the Pyrenees Mountains until arriving at Santiago de Compostela only a short distance from the Atlantic Ocean the opposite side of the Iberian Peninsula. The Camino is an ancient pilgrimage path attracting the faithful, and otherwise, from a variety of thoughts and circumstances, the world over. Nevertheless, many Peregrinos I met on the way had often journeyed from countries sharing in a Catholic religious tradition.

I returned to the Camino two years later in April, 2006 where time was spent exploring places of historical interest and enjoying the company of what some might describe as eccentric characters.

Early on in my second Camino and while walking up a hill in the French Pyrenees I met an Englishman. A bohemian type character who claimed to be not only a Buddhist but one of the last pupils at Eton public school to be flogged - in 1962 or thereabouts. We shared anecdotes, cigars and red wine before I moved on and off the beaten track to find the Church of Saint Mary Eunate, a 12th century, and some say a Knights Templar Church, octagonal in design with a three-sided apse.

On this visit I noticed that flowers adorned the Romanesque arched entrance. Inside there was barely room for twenty people but the atmosphere was one of immense quiet and stillness whereupon further journeys were contemplated. After a hundred more miles of walking I finally left the Camino to visit Salamanca, Avilla and, Cordoba.

Spring in Cordoba is a splendid time to visit the botanical gardens, designed in a harmonious rectangular arrangement of low rosemary hedges, fountains and regal looking statues adjacent to an orange grove and, further on, to some stunning architecture particularly with regard to views found inside the Mosque-Cathedral. And, in a nearby plaza, one can find a statue of a Roman stoic philosopher and statesman whose words inspired a short piece titled, *Freedom*.

I digress, but on occasion diversions can be fruitful which I hope is both a feature and a reward for time taken reading this autobiographical collection of essays and opinions of a life lived differently; an archetypal example, *A Night Out in Oxford* – The epilogue.

Camino Rebirth

"Thereby hangs a tale." Shakespeare.

E arly one morning walking across Spain I stopped to eat a croissant and coffee somewhere on the outskirts of Burgos. After getting up to continue my journey I noticed on the other side of the plaza, a young, fairly tall, slim woman venturing in the same direction and carrying not only a large rucksack but that sense of purpose people have when out walking to a destination a long way away.

We walked at a similar pace for a while so I made conversation and this continued until we stopped some fifteen or twenty miles later at a sign which informed of a place to stay about a kilometre off the beaten track (but feeling much further after a day walking in the heat of the sun), so we decided that it was time to seek some rest and investigate.

I heard a woman singing a German song reminiscent of something from a 1940's film. It was then that I noticed an old record player and two young gay Germans standing nearby. They introduced themselves in English explaining that they ran the show and what would we like for dinner?

After spending a day in the sun it was exhilarating to find an alburgue - which is a name for a Spanish youth hostel equipped for travellers on the Camino - an ancient pilgrimage route across northern Spain, which attracts people from all over the world who want to experience something different for a multitude of reasons.

This alburgue, however, was unusually inviting. On arrival it was made known that guests could expect the following refreshments; dinner with red wine in the evening, an ample sized well-made hammock strung between two tall trees, and a large stone bath situated in the garden near, but not beneath, a procession of trees identifying the perimeter of the grounds.

It was now late afternoon. In the canopy of the trees leaves gently rustled as an occasional cool breeze changed direction. I dived into the cold water of the stone bath, not forgetting to first remove a grubby t-shirt and shorts, and subsequently sat on the stone edge eyeing the only hammock available and wondering when it would be vacated by the enigmatic French girl who had become my travelling companion for the past ten hours.

She was by now happily submerged in a book and I very much doubted whether she would ever vacate the hammock which looked increasingly attractive the less chance I had of using it, so I slipped back into the idiosyncratic delights of immersing a fatigued body in freezing cold water.

It was in this relaxing informal scene that I eventually noticed an empty hammock and so pulled myself out of the water, quickly dried, dressed and finally, contentedly, climbed into the, by now, swinging hammock.

I gazed up at a peaceful sky interrupted only by branches of tall trees swaying in the wind. My imagination wandered and I thought about the journey I had made from Roncesvalles on the border of France.

I had arrived in Bilbao some weeks beforehand and then quickly left for San Sebastian where, after finding myself locked out of my room at 1.00am, decided to sleep on the beach, waking-up in the morning to find the Bay of Biscay only a few inches from my feet.

Thereupon I had taken a bus to Pamplona where, in an old hotel room, dreams turned to nightmares, and then into cold sweats, and finally into an epiphany. After waking-up I felt compelled to resign from a career as a successful sales representative for a prestigious English publishing company. I sent an email with my resignation. I felt a huge wave of relief sweep through my body.

Thoughts continued, I noticed a bird fly overhead while I remained in the hammock. I mulled over in my mind another decision to head for the old Spanish monastery at Roncesvalles which began this journey and the walk to Santiago de Compostela. It was something I had previously only read about, but after listening to my soul, I fully understood what had to be done. This was my story and I began to feel more and more comfortable with it, but what about the French girl. What was her story?

I never did find out the answer until a month after returning from the Camino. We had finally parted company further on and nearer to Santiago when accommodation becomes scarcer as the number of pilgrims increases the demand for somewhere to sleep. We eventually found a place but there was room for only one.

I wondered what to do while the French girl talked with the person responsible for accommodation. They were talking animatedly in French and Spanish. I glanced at the French girl and saw a face revealing some duress and agitation so was not completely surprised when it became apparent that I was left to search alone for somewhere to stay.

In desperation I went to a bar for a meal and a drink hoping for some kind of deliverance, which arrived in the form of an Italian family at the next table who kindly offered me a floor for the night. This meant I could continue with my Camino, but what about that French girl. What happened to her?

Post-Camino, back in England and some four weeks after leaving Spain, I received a package in the post. It contained a book, a letter, and a photograph. It was from the French girl.

The book, a modern novel, I never did read. The letter, however, informed me that she had had a baby, and the picture of a newborn smiling baby confirmed it.

The Coach Trip

So we all piled into our respective coaches. It was 7.00am and a five-hour journey lay ahead. We were travelling to the mountains, then up and into the mountains, and further on still until reaching a city with a cable car system. Destination unknown.

A few days beforehand teachers were informed by management that there would be a day off on Thursday (a change in the law meant that the weekend became Friday and Saturday instead of Thursday and Friday) and that on this day we were invited to go on a coach trip with our students on a sort of bonding exercise. I had no idea where exactly we were heading. Neither did anyone else. Perhaps the driver knew. I hoped so.

Early on Thursday morning I met up with some other teachers downstairs in the hotel lobby at 6.00am. I wore my blue linen shirt, sunglasses and beige British style hat which suggested holiday rather than work. I felt relaxed and enjoyed another chance to explore somewhere different. I had no idea of where we were going. All I knew was that this was a trip arranged by the company that employed me and that teachers were expected to accompany students on a coach journey. Anticipation, as well as the ever present sand and dust hung in the air while waiting to leave from our starting point which was some waste ground situated in front of the makeshift workplace building where we taught English to Saudi nationals. They were young men of mixed English language ability mainly aged about twenty to twenty-five years old.

I sat down in an empty seat. Behind me sat an American teacher. We talked for the duration of the journey as did two different sets of students on a sixty-seat coach. We sometimes seemed to drift past unfamiliar landscapes as the noise of the coach engine competed with the laughter of students.

My American colleague and I spoke about music and I was surprised to learn that his knowledge of 1970's and 80's rock bands was better than my own. We talked more on the gigs we attended until the subject of music faded and stories about past work experiences grew. Meanwhile, the scenery outside, unlike the conversation, changed from semi-desert to rock.

We then talked about places we had been and so I mentioned an artistic-themed trip from my past, which led to exploring a Pyrenean cave due South of Carcassonne in France. I explained the details of a journey; begun in London via Paris, visiting art galleries and cafes near the river Seine, and then on by train to Toulouse, Carcassonne, and the beautiful town of Foix, noted for its impressive castle which stands upon a large rock.

I remembered buying a bottle of red wine, tomatoes, cheese and bread from the local market and thinking that the quality of the taste is what I might expect from the Queen's former grocer, Harrods, yet the price was affordable to peasants. I recalled seeing a poster advertising a nearby cave, telling my travel companion of that time about it, and finding a taxi to explore further.

Deep down inside the darkness of this enormous cave, I saw the incredible Paleolithic artwork of pre-historic Man; of bison, deer and birds in shades of brown, black and white. It was astonishing to see how these forms appeared framed by the diameters of this subterranean space.

Reminiscences and conversation helped to pass the time and five hours quickly came and went until we arrived at our hitherto unknown destination; a city in the mountains of south-west Saudi Arabia. From the coach it was possible to see the worn façade of a beige coloured building containing a number of cable cars. It was cloudy and threatened to rain.

We got off the coach and into a throng of people waiting to get into the building. Once inside, a cable car beckoned and we looked on as students filled the first empty carriages which swung round onto the platform.

At last a carriage arrived which had my name on it. I got on and was followed by about seven other teachers. Then the doors closed automatically and we were off, suspended in mid-air by what I suspected was dated European technology. Gliding past the few remaining teachers on the platform we began to descend into a very large valley. It was possible to see different forms of wildlife below although whatever others noticed I didn't see. My focus was on what lay ahead rather than what was beneath.

We continued to descend deeper into the valley until the cable car and its carriage of baffled colleagues slid into the terminus. I had anticipated getting off. This place looked interesting. But the thought passed almost as quickly as the opportunity. The carriage swiftly turned in and around on its projected course and up and away into mid-air returning whence it came. I was speechless.

Others appeared less astonished at this sudden turn of events. I thought they might know something I didn't so I, not wishing to appear uninformed, said nothing. Glumly I surveyed the increasing distance between the cable car and the conurbation below which became smaller by the second.

So up we went until arriving back where we began some thirty minutes beforehand. I got off the cable car and joined the large crowd of students and colleagues. We jostled for position while seeking the coach for the return journey. Back in my seat I thought more on this journey and why we had travelled some two hundred miles into the mountains just to sit in a cable car for thirty minutes? This question, as intriguing as it is, remains unanswered.

It was then that I considered that those representing my London based employer were mad. They might pay a decent salary, but it came at a price. The workplace was fraught with hostility and intimidation. I was expected to do two jobs simultaneously and there were not enough hours in the day to complete them.

I had signed up to teach but it seemed that half my time was taken up with administrative tasks which were increasingly stressful because the demands of perfection were changed by management every week. My mind drifted and I began to think of a route to a saner world when I did not have to work for someone else.

After some while it was time to disembark for something to eat. We were directed into a ground-floor building with a squat looking tower, teachers and students filed through a maze of corridors until emerging into a large area reminiscent of a medieval English banquet hall, except without a large log fire and women.

We duly sat on one side of a long rectangular table and waited to be served rice, vegetables and tender spicy, on the bone, lamb. The atmosphere was not unpleasant but neither did any of us appear fully relaxed.

Thereafter, some time was spent outside near the coaches chatting with students who took the opportunity to take photographs of teachers. Subsequently, a timely moment was taken lying in the sun, which had at last broken through the mountainous clouds. I chatted amongst friends for a while longer and took a few pictures before getting back on the coach to continue the final leg of the return journey to our arid town not far from Yemen.

The coach wound its way downwards through the mountains. The sky became darker. We stopped suddenly and someone asked in Arabic for a sheet of paper. I was confident that everyone was present and correct when handing over the paper containing the names of everyone on board. Someone ran over to the tiny Police station hut and returned after ten minutes. We had permission to drive on.

We set off once again winding our way further and further down until reaching the semi-desert plain below, but coaches following after would not be as fortunate and were ordered by the Police to remain where they were parked for hours until detailed security checks had been made.

My American friend was now on the coach with his students. He would be lucky to be back before midnight. Never change a horse in mid-stream, I thought.

My coach arrived at 8.30pm. It had been an unusual day and I was glad to have made it back in one piece. Others arrived later still and some did not arrive back until almost midnight, which is what I had expected.

Slumped on a small couch in the lounge drinking a hot mug of Yunnan black tea, I had been back in my hotel apartment for several hours when I heard my neighbour, the Aussie teacher next-door, exit the lift, sigh, swear, open and then slam his front door shut. It was the end of a long journey home.

Mud bunging

A boyhood quest; for the perfect stick, the best clay, and the perfect throw.

When summers were long and the days hazy it was decided that we should go *mud bunging*. Who thought up this activity no one knew and, quite honestly, no one cared. This was a moment when, unlike adults, we knew exactly what we wanted to do and if this meant flinging some mud across the lake at someone else then all well and good. In retrospect, this is much like the behaviour of adults; so call it an apprenticeship, if you like.

The idea of going *mud bunging* would sometimes arrive while lying on the bank of a nearby lake. Or, the notion might occur after partaking in some *reed boat* making activity which meant tearing the top of a reed - which was often found in amongst the bulrushes - and then folding the reed over itself into the shape of a circle.

By placing the tip of the reed carefully into a small cut made with a fingernail at the base it was possible to recreate the keel of a boat. Thus converting a reed into what we called, *a reed boat*. Construction took a minute or two but once accomplished it was time to proceed.

A reed, once made into a boat, was placed in the lake. This intricate task was accomplished every so often by lying face down on a sloping earth bank towards the lake and with an outstretched arm fingers could position a reed so that it lightly touched the surface of the water. Too much pressure and the reed would sink, sometimes without trace. If successful, a reed would float but it would take a gust of wind for it to sail well.

NO SACRED OXEN

Depending on the strength of the wind an archetypal reed boat could make good progress and sail at speeds approaching one knot. Some boats were known to have sunk when hit by a large piece of mud. The wind decided when this race would begin and sometimes patience was stretched to the limit and sometimes there was no wind at all. It was at times like this that we went *mud bunging*.

Mud bunging meant finding a thin stick, preferably a yard long and firm yet also pliable. To test the suitability one had to pretend it was a whip and listen for a familiar sound as a long narrow object hit air at speed. If we heard a sharp *swish* sound it was likely to be chosen as a *mud bunger*.

Arming oneself with a decent mud bunger often signified that the first stage was over. Not infrequently I found an acceptable stick at the bottom of my road in amongst the bushes. I could then turn to the business of finding the best clay for the job of throwing mud at my friends.

With a bendy stick in hand we returned to the bank beside the lake and jumped down into an area affording access to clay with, as we thought it, the right amount of moisture. Not too hard, nor too soft. Not too sticky either, otherwise the mud wouldn't leave the stick. Occasionally, this happened and might be considered similar in effect to someone firing a blank from a gun. Our aim was not as precise or as lethal but a similar principle applied and we stuck to it.

The clay was usually various shades of brown, although now and then I noticed hues of blue which almost had the texture of putty and a consistency which offered the maximum effect for mud gripping the top of the stick until the force of casting the stick - in the same manner as a fisherman casts his rod - forces the mud by sheer momentum to leave the top of the stick where the clay had been meticulously applied. Note that I use the terms mud and clay interchangeably.

Battle ensued when all the preliminaries had been accomplished. Looking back on it, half the fun was the preparation. Young minds were focused on achieving something and it was creative. Depending on the numbers available, three or four of us would wander to the bank on the far side of the lake with a stick and supplies of mud in hand. Once willing combatants were embedded on opposite sides of the lake hostilities could begin.

Have you ever seen Kenneth Branagh's film, Henry V? A scene that readily springs to mind is a moment immediately prior to the clash of English and French armies; the sky is a quiver of arrows. Well, it was nothing like that, but there were times when six or seven pieces of mud were seen soaring through the air over the lake simultaneously and was a glorious sight to behold. Reloading set the pulse racing – it was important to get a good grip – and I was confident in getting through quite a bit of ammunition.

Accuracy was also important but it must be admitted that this had as much to do with luck as judgment. A hit was a tremendous thing bringing about lots of laughter, especially upon hearing the impact of mud against forehead. Sound travels quickly across water. More often than not traces of mud peppered jackets and jeans - identifying battle scars for some and badges of honour for others.

Not infrequently someone might lose his footing and carelessly get a sock or shoe wet, this was known as *a bootie*. More merriment. Delight at others' suffering was a feature of my boyhood and not confined to my amusement alone.

As for the wildlife on the water in the lake; swans, coots, ducks, moorhens, all of it went over their heads. Hostilities ended when the supply of ammunition ran out. A favourite stick was kept in the garden and further supplies of clay remained in the bank. Future battles beckoned.

Like an eagle in Oman

Throwing oneself off a rock ledge ninety-two feet high does not sound like fun unless you happened to be in Wadi Shab, a large canyon-type valley located near the coast between the cities, Sur and Muscat, in Oman in late September 2012. It was from this perspective that contestant and spectator viewed events from a variety of vantage points that converge into a narrow pass one very hot and sunny afternoon.

In the manner of a champion, Gary Hunt, waved to the crowd below. Wearing very little apart from red swimming trunks and a broad smile, Gary regained his composure and stood upright, if somewhat precariously, on the edge of the board and the abyss below. People looked up to him. It was essential for the crowd to allow divers some brief moments to collect their thoughts and concentrate on the complexity of the dive about to be enacted. The tension grew and silence descended before he did. Seconds passed, before Gary suddenly leapt off the fixed Red Bull board and into the hot afternoon air. Now approaching one hundred feet, he quickly plunged straight down performing twists and turns and three somersaults – a triple quad, an innovative dive rarely attempted. Almost immediately, Gary's streamlined body entered the naturally deep rock pool at the base of the cliff without a discernible splash. A clean entry into the water and a degree of difficulty of 6.3 made it a superb dive for the competition and a memorable spectacle for everyone else.

I waited a while for the winner to be declared and left soon after hearing that England's, Gary Hunt, was indeed the Cliff Diving Champion for 2012. It was not a huge surprise, but it took courage. Alone he did it.

There was a ship

The moving moon went up the sky,
And nowhere did abide:
Softly she was going up,
And a star or two beside –

During the process of writing emerged a deep truth about myself. In July 1981 I went with a friend on a trip around Europe. We had planned to fly to Athens and visit a Greek island but I had second thoughts and decided that I would rather travel by train and this led to a journey to France, Germany, Italy and Switzerland instead.

My travel companion, a budding union representative and Chelsea fan, took with him a book to read on the train, *Tess of the d'Urbervilles*, by Thomas Hardy. I did not take anything to read. I was happy to sit and stare at an ever-changing view.

In Paris I had the best croissant and coffee followed by the best beer in Koblenz. As we travelled further by train through Switzerland it was possible to see the beauty of the scenery and mountains, the grass valleys and splendid homes in perfect isolation before finally reaching our immediate destination, the Italian beach resort of Rimini, popular with Germans, but strangely empty when we arrived.

Our accommodation was basic and next to an outhouse and garden of washing lines and drying clothes. Inside a shared room I wrote a letter to my then girlfriend back in London. I had tried unsuccessfully to end the relationship one evening near Victoria Station. I thought it might be best to avoid any complications resulting from my soon-to-be departure.

But she cried and I felt bad. At the time I lacked the resolve to take things to a necessary conclusion. It would be another two years before we finally parted for good.

Apart from a swim and lying on a beach there was little to do in Rimini. There were plenty of empty bars selling German beer and some might think sun, sea and good quality German beer enough. For a few days it was until we set off for Rome where all roads and some trains lead. On arrival it seemed as if we had appeared in a very large outdoor museum.

Perhaps the most visibly impressive attraction of what is left of this Roman world is the Colosseum. Inside and underneath in a maze of tunnels and catacombs it is easier to imagine the events which once took place in this ancient stadium where gladiators waited to dispatch and be dispatched. Later that evening, in a Rome restaurant, I dispatched the best thin, crusty, pizza.

In another part of Rome we visited Vatican City and St Peter's Church. I was amazed at how vast the interior of the Church looked. My surprise was not simply about the size of the Basilica but its peaceful stillness and its sublime art and beauty. Not knowing what else to see I wandered around and waited in the sunshine for my friend in St. Peter's Square. It was not that crowded. He told me that he had been to see the Sistine Chapel. I asked him what he was talking about and he said something about it being an important place to see. I had never heard of it and felt disappointed that no one had ever told me about it. I expected knowledge to come to me rather than search for it, which I did ten years later by taking a degree in Theology. This enabled me to ask hundreds of questions and listen to some informed answers.

The rest was for me to consider and evaluate but I enjoyed being a mature student and learning at a time when most men are providing for families or establishing their careers.

NO SACRED OXEN

Our train left Rome for Switzerland. Like St Peter's, it was not modern and was all the more enjoyable for that. I walked along a narrow passageway and opened a carriage window as we rumbled along. I breathed in the warm air and returned to my seat. My friend, sitting immediately opposite, had arrived at the last few pages of *Tess of the d'Urbervilles*. I knew little or nothing about this tragic story until after finishing my studies in Oxford when I became absorbed in reading more of the imagined world of Thomas Hardy.

We continued on and up to the Alps eventually arriving through and down onto the northern plain where the capital of Switzerland is situated. Berne is some distance away from the Alps and magical shades of blue and white were clearly visible on the summer's day horizon.

I wandered around the city after having sorted out the accommodation. My friend did similarly. We would meet up later in the evening. It was by now early afternoon and had already explored an arcade of shops when I found a wooden bench near a main clock tower. I noticed that up above located somewhere near the clock was a circular parade of small moving figures activated by some mechanical device within the clock and possibly corresponding to the hour. The sun shone brightly although not quite as hot as it had been in Rome. I sat and considered the atmosphere and the view. At an angle to my left I became aware of an attractive looking young woman about my age. I spoke first. Being English I said something about the weather. We talked more and arranged to meet up the next day.

In the evening I returned to the pension to meet up with my friend and made plans for the evening and resulted in a visit to a local friendly atmospheric hostelry featuring a guitarist and songs sung by anyone who knew the words. Tomorrow, however, beckoned.

NO SACRED OXEN

We met again in the centre of town and walked to the park where we talked and I discovered that in Swiss German my surname meant horse. We subsequently returned to whence we came and explored other places hitherto unknown by me. A type of public balcony overlooking an outdoor swimming pool comes to mind. The sun shone brightly and we took each other's photograph on my camera. Later I discussed the latest turn of events with my friend who said that he wanted to leave and return home to England.

The following afternoon I went for a walk wondering what to do and stopped at a bus stop arriving at a conclusion that I would return with my friend and this would bring this holiday romance to an end. But I found this decision more difficult than I expected. I was unsure about whether this was the right thing to do. Still, I had to make a decision so I let my friend know I would be leaving with him. That same evening I met my new girlfriend for the last time.

We kissed and talked more on the steps of a church and she implored me to keep her address safe in the small red plastic container emblazoned with the Swiss flag now affectionately tied around my neck. The next morning I left for a train to Dieppe where my friend and I would continue our journey home by ferry across the English Channel to Dover.

On board the ship I looked back at the trail of the wake of the sea as the ship moved further way from France and closer to England. My thoughts returned to Switzerland.

I had never expected to meet someone I wanted to be with. Somehow my thinking viewed this as a problem rather than the affirmation of something wonderful. I thought of my now two girlfriends. This was not a situation I could tolerate. Some are able to juggle emotional relationships but I was not able to do this. Even the cross-over period between choosing one or the other revealed more about my own emotional immaturity than it did about the wisdom or otherwise of any choice made. I stood on the deck of the ship as it sped further and further towards the coast of England. My emotions considered thoughts and my thoughts considered conflicting emotions. I had no idea what to do. I was not able to resolve the questions that leapt from my mind. Suddenly I ripped off the gift from around my neck, held it in my hand and, in despair, flung it into the sea. I resolved that I would later destroy the film which contained pictures of the Swiss girl since I knew that if I saw her again, even a picture, I would have to contact her and this would mean feeling emotional confusion all over again. Strangely, my action of throwing away her address had not made me any happier.

> *I looked upon the rotting sea,*
> *And drew my eyes away;*
> *I looked upon the rotting deck,*
> *And there the dead men lay.*
>
> *I looked to heaven and tried to pray ;*
> *But or ever a prayer had gusht,*
> *A wicked whisper came, and made*
> *My heart as dry as dust.*

Back in London I destroyed the camera film containing evidence of my happiness in Berne. I thought it the right thing to do. I already had a girlfriend.

This relationship would have to finish before I found another. This evaluation was some consolation until I met a mate whom I had known since boyhood. His parents' home backed onto mine. We talked over the garden fence.

He asked me about my time travelling round Europe by train? I told him that it had been great and that I had met a beautiful girl in Switzerland. *Did I have a photograph?* He asked. No, I said. I explained that I already had a girlfriend and that I thought it best to get rid of the picture. He stared at me in bemusement and disappointment, not for himself, but for me. I realized then what I had done.

> *Alone, alone, all, all alone,*
> *Alone on a wide wide sea!*
> *And never a saint took pity on*
> *My soul in agony.*

It was not until writing recently, however, that I became aware of the import of *The Rime of the Ancient Mariner* by Samuel Taylor Coleridge and its significance in my life. I had killed the albatross. The poem ends with a message of divine hope; salvation is found through the telling of this story. If thereafter you can touch the core of your being without it feeling bruised that is something very special indeed.

> *He prayeth best, who loveth best*
> *All things both great and small;*
> *For the dear God who loveth us,*
> *He made and loveth all.*

What is the difference?

Thou art a scholar, speak to it Horatio.
Shakespeare

Sometimes students ask me whether there are any differences between themselves and students from other countries?

It is an interesting question. Chinese students are often enthusiastic and diligent although I recall a few memorable exceptions. On one occasion, at a private school located in the coastal city of Ningbo, a particularly troublesome student attracted the attention of a Chinese teacher walking past my classroom prior to the start of a lesson. She stormed into the classroom to remonstrate with this student although I had decided to tolerate his behavior until after registration when the class had time to settle down.

The door had burst open and in strode a middle-aged woman. She went straight up to the noisy student and slapped him across the face, kicked his shin, and then kneed him in the stomach. And for good measure the student was left with a volley of abuse. She left as quickly as she had arrived and slammed the door behind her and the class was now deafeningly silent.

The fifteen-year old boy was subdued for a while but his spirits eventually lifted and in subsequent lessons he was rarely as troublesome again. This was an exception, however, and student/teacher relations were characteristically conducted without incident and with mutual respect.

One of the most enjoyable teaching experiences was during lessons with first year university students in Dalian who loved to learn. Chinese students, mostly girls, listened studiously and were keen to partake in any instructive classroom activities.

In fact, girls in China, Thailand and Oman, more often than not, outperformed boys in their attentiveness and ability to learn the English language. Generally speaking, however, there were more similarities than differences and this is true in my experience of teaching.

For instance, boys in Oman can be as uninterested in learning a foreign language as boys from Thailand. Conversely, girls from China can be as enthusiastic as girls from Oman although there will be cultural differences in expressing their interest.

I recall teaching in the historical desert town of Ibri, in Oman, a predominately female class aged about eighteen years of age who were a delight to teach. One girl sat at the front with an infectious beaming smile while others responded dutifully and positively to a variety of class activities. It is at such times that teaching is most rewarding for student and teacher alike.

In Saudi Arabia my class consisted of young men in their early twenties. I was fortunate in that this class was more enthusiastic and more of a team than other classes nearby. When students were asked to do something – I explained how certain tasks would enhance an understanding of English - the class focused on what needed to be accomplished.

We all got on well and their successful collective performance in the end of term exams and assessments was, I think, a reflection of hard work and a positive attitude.

My experience of teaching in Saudi Arabia was not always so positive but this had nothing to do with the students who were a great bunch of lads. So what is the difference between students from different cultures and nations?

NO SACRED OXEN

I suppose there are obvious differences in the difficulties of pronunciation and in appearance, for example, in the way people look especially when one group of people wear some form of religious dress code while others do not.

Returning to the initial question, students can and do reflect national differences but in the classroom these differences either do not matter or provide a reason to celebrate the uniqueness of peoples around the world.

Personally, I would rather visit different countries in order to experience diversity rather than see the laws of the land changed in my own country in order to accommodate the invidious political agenda of homegrown multiculturalism.

The diversity of people and culture in this world is a cause for celebration but it is not for a political elite to play with traditional views of cultural identity in order to stake their overweening claims to the moral high ground. If people prefer their own indigenous culture while at the same time enjoying the experience of living and working abroad I see nothing wrong with that. Indeed, I recommend it.

Classroom teaching in the East and Middle East has provided a certain perspective on these things and I feel privileged to have had an opportunity to engage with students confident in their own country and culture rather than as immigrants or migrants. It is an experience I believe has afforded me a unique insight, not only into differences, but has underlined the similarities and what people have in common. When I travel and teach in other countries and cultures I have often found a world not yet burdened with the same measure of guilt and shame dished out liberally by those who practise unthinking conformity with prevailing fashion at the cost of a once great nation which has created the world's most popular language.

Auf dem Weg nach Berlin

So there we all sat on the four-hour road trip from Bremen to Berlin by taxi. Three Germans and an Englishman.

I had to be in Berlin to visit a few more universities where English is used for teaching and then return to England. My job was to meet up with lecturers to discuss the merits of a selection of academic books which amounted to a portfolio of published titles which introduced the relevance or otherwise for any particular course.

I represented an English publisher keen to increase sales in this foreign field and, aware of how expense accounts were sometimes carefully scrutinized, considered it economical to take a shared taxi instead of a train or plane to Berlin. Besides, this mode of travel was different from the usual scheme of things and this has always attracted my attention. To secure a place in a shared taxi it is necessary to make some plans. I visited a locally based agency and waited to be notified of where and when to turn up for the trip to Berlin.

For a nominal fee a passenger is notified via email or phone of a driver who has spare room in their car and is travelling to the same destination or somewhere on the way. It is early in the morning. I arrive at the designated spot. I find the car taxi waiting a short distance from where I expect it to be, and after a moment's hesitation, get in and introduce myself while paying the driver petrol money.

I am seated in the front beside the driver and the three of us are waiting for the last passenger to arrange his luggage in the back of the car. In the background proprietors can be heard opening up the shutters of shop windows. Meanwhile, further introductions are made and then we set off on to the autobahn and Berlin.

NO SACRED OXEN

Two laconic-minded passengers sit in the back. Fortunately, the driver is talkative and this breaks the teutonic ice. The car taxi service was, at the time of my visit in Autumn 2003, a popular method of transport, it saved money and it was a good way to meet people. Moreover, the car owner could feel that he was providing some benefit to the community or the environment. It soon became apparent, however, that the passengers in the back had not come for a chat. I asked the driver about his reasons for driving to Berlin?

He explains that he often makes this trip and it could become monotonous so he liked to invite people along. I soon realized after engaging in more conversation that the driver sitting beside me is a member of a rock band. What is more his band were well-known in Germany but particularly in Berlin where he was expected to perform later in the week. We had left Bremen thirty minutes before but I realized that the driver had been on the road for much of his life. He spoke excellent English and fitted the bill in clothes, manner and character. He liked the Rolling Stones and reminded me of a German equivalent of Mick Jagger, although this might have had something to do with a man who, like me, was no longer young. I learn more about the band and the driver's fame as we speed past unmemorable scenery on either side of the autobahn when it becomes apparent that our discussion about German rock music has reached a final encore.

Time passes and German is spoken which breaks the silence. A few minutes afterwards the car taxi pulls up at a convenient point and one of the passengers in the back opens the door and, without ceremony, quickly disembarks.

The three of us continue on our way and the silence continued until the driver remembers it is his father's birthday. He tells me that if his father were alive today he would have been one hundred years old. The driver glances across at me to see whether I might be interested in hearing more? It was a prescient moment.

He explains that he was one of eight children. His father had married late in life and died some twenty years before, but what he wanted to talk about was an episode in the life of his father during WW2. He was an officer in the German army at Stalingrad in 1942 and was stationed in a train carriage where he worked and slept. As a cartographer in the Wehrmacht it was his job to make maps useful for military campaigns and these skills would one day enable him to leave Stalingrad at an opportune moment.

In the autumn of 1942 the war was going badly for the Germans. The Sixth Army Group consisting of some six hundred thousand men were bottled up in Stalingrad and stiff Russian resistance meant that soldiers faced the bleak prospect of death or a Russian winter. The cartographer in the train carriage had seen the writing on the wall and the blood on the ground and with the assistance of a fellow officer made plans for escape.

Documents and papers were copied and forged but some overwhelming reason for leaving Stalingrad was vital for any chance of success. It was not entirely clear to me how the two men in the train carriage took possession of a dead General, but then again, dead Generals were not so rare in Stalingrad and the availability of this one kept the plan on track. The dead General was going to be used as a proxy for leaving Stalingrad.

It was absolutely necessary for forms to look authentic and painstaking work went into making official orders originating from German high command appear as genuine as possible. The forged papers informed the reader that the dead General's body was to be transferred to the safety of German defensive positions, several hundred kilometers away to the West. Amidst the bombs and machine gun fire and hell of Stalingrad it would be worth trying something, however implausible, to get out.

A chance moment arrived and the high-ranking corpse was lifted into the motorbike side-car, a machine gun remained firmly fixed on the front of the beige three-wheeled vehicle. The two escapees got onto the motorbike one behind the other. The BMW engine roared into life but a German checkpoint lay immediately ahead. This would prove to be a far-reaching test of their nerve and their cartographic skills.

Soldiers at the checkpoint observed the strange figure of a lifeless uniformed General. The two officers were asked to show papers and confirmed that indeed the body was to be transported to an area behind German lines. It was an incredulous order but this official document confirmed it. Without further impediment they set off for the vast Ukrainian plain and a perilous journey ahead.

Some distance was travelled without incident when a Russian sniper hit the pillion passenger - the father of the taxi driver - in the back. Despite this and in having little other alternative they drove on through *No man's land* until finally reaching their goal of the German defensive position. There must have been astonishment at the sight of the incoming motorbike but orders verified the reason for its arrival.

With the dead General safely delivered the two men left German occupied Soviet Union for Berlin. The taxi driver's father went to hospital where he remained for months and subsequently played no further part in the war, but at least the two friends had escaped from Stalingrad and both had survived.

At this moment, the teller of the story, the taxi driver, arrived at the outskirts of Berlin. We had been travelling for nearly four hours and for the last half of it I had spent my time listening or reflecting on the words spoken as we ventured further on our journey. We slowed down to take in the view of converging lanes; the driver explained that years before he and hundreds, perhaps thousands of others in their vehicles, routinely waited at this point for hours or even days while East German communist soldiers closely examined passports or identity documents. But now, since the collapse of communism in Germany and the removal of the Berlin Wall we could proceed without any such formalities.

As we continued into the centre of Berlin I heard the remaining part of this tale. His father had kept in touch with his friend after the war and both had married local German women at approximately the same time. They lived in the same town and remained close friends thereafter. One morning, after many years had passed, the driver's mother telephoned her friend with some sad news. *Hans is dead*, she said. The woman at the other end of the phone line listened intently, then replied: *Sven also died this morning*. The two men who had experienced so much life together died within a minute or two of each other in their nearby homes.

Our conversation had come to an end and so had our journey from Bremen. I looked around me and saw we had arrived amid the sparse crowds and wide streets of Berlin.

An ode to sadness: Keats reading in Wentworth Place

A posthumous portrait of John Keats, the romantic poet, hangs in the National Portrait Gallery in London. Keats is shown to be in a mood of deep contemplation in the tranquility of an early afternoon of Georgian Hampstead.

What Keats is reading is unknown. What we do know is that the portrait was completed by his close friend, Joseph Severn in 1823, a few years after the death of Keats in Rome when Joseph Severn is said to have tenderly ministered to the spiritual and physical needs of the dying poet.

The picture of Keats reveals an unusual portrait of Shakespeare, which can be seen hanging on the wall and is thought by some to be a depiction of a young Shakespeare with a full head of hair. This picture was given to Keats by a landlady while staying on the Isle of Wight a year or so beforehand and is said to have inspired some of his later writing, although the artist of the Shakespeare portrait remains unknown.

Back to the portrait of John Keats where we find him sitting on a chair with his left elbow resting on one side of another chair with fingers on his head as if attempting to touch thought. Formally attired in black and white, Keats is enveloped, like his later life, by hues of brown.

In the background and to one side, is a view of a garden scene through a large open window of contrasting green, blue and white complementing a sense of peacefulness and stillness. This portrait continues to fascinate and is an inspirational reason to visit Keats House, formerly known as Wentworth Place in Hampstead.

NO SACRED OXEN

It was, therefore, with this in mind that I asked a friend with more knowledge of Keats than myself, to accompany me on a visit to Hampstead.

On arrival at Keats House we met a friendly and helpful guide whose enthusiasm for his subject increased in his telling of stories; a delight for most with an interest in knowing more about the life of Keats. Interest was heightened, however, by the appearance and manner of our guide who reminded us of an archetypal Dickensian clerk from the novel *Bleak House*.

Our Dickensian guide – describing himself as a volunteer - mused on things historical while answering questions since forgotten, but we learnt much and my appreciation of Keats has become all the greater because of it.

The first two verses of *Ode to a Nightingale* follow. It is said that Keats wrote this poem at Wentworth Place (now, Keats House) in 1819 when, as a former medical student at Guy's hospital, he would have been fully aware of his failing health.

My heart aches, and a drowsy numbness pains
My sense, as though of hemlock I had drunk,
Or emptied some dull opiate to the drains
One minute past, and Lethe-wards had sunk:
Tis not through envy of thy happy lot,
But being too happy in thine happiness,
That thou, light-winged Dryad of the trees
In some melodious plot
Of beechen green, and shadows numberless,
Singest of summer in full-throated ease.

O, for a draught of vintage! that hath been
Cool'd a long age in the deep-delved earth,
Tasting of Flora and the country green,
Dance, and Provençal song, and sunburnt mirth!

NO SACRED OXEN

O for a beaker full of the warm South,
Full of the true, the blushful Hippocrene,
With beaded bubbles winking at the brim,
And purple-stained mouth;
That I might drink, and leave the world unseen,
And with thee fade away into the forest dim:

Wolf-like peregrinations

On the Camino in the summer of 2004 I met a German by the name of Wolf. He was in charge of an alburgue or youth hostel in Mansilla a few miles prior to Leon where in the centre of the city stands an imposing Cathedral with a huge array of impressively colourful stained glass windows. It had taken nearly three weeks to arrive in Mansilla and here, while signing in my name and passing over my Peregrino passbook for a stamp to confirm my attendance, I expectantly anticipated treatment for a toe, which invariably ached. I had injured it a few decades before doing Judo at the Budokwai in London. After walking for several hundred miles or more my toe began to ache and distract from the enjoyment of the scenery, which had so often delighted.

It was in this setting, in a open air ground level hall or courtyard, that I waited in a queue of sorts talking with other people about their Camino experiences and hoping that something could be done to alleviate the pain which was beginning to impede the progress of my journey westwards across this undulating ancient path of pilgrimage. It was here that most, but not all, hoped for healing.

A woman from Barcelona left almost as quickly as she had arrived. I remembered a conversation after leaving Pamplona several weeks beforehand on a hill with a commanding view and occupied by an ice cream van, a collection of large shapes and figures sculptured from rusting metal, and a collection of ubiquitous wind turbines just outside the city.

I saw her waiting for a bus to return to Barcelona and heard her say something about a bad leg and being unable to continue further. A friendly Spanish bloke from Malaga - who I had chatted with at various times on the Camino but had latterly overtaken me - explained that he had developed tendonitis, an inflammation of the Achilles tendon, and that this had slowed him down.

Neither Spaniards from Barcelona or Malaga respectively were seeking treatment from Wolf. They did not believe in unconventional medical cures. I was amazed. Why not try it and find out for yourself instead of struggling on for another three or four hundred miles? In a way I admired his determination to carry on but thought it barmy to do so without taking advantage of a once in a lifetime moment.

I knew my decision and hoped for healing. I had nothing to lose. If it didn't work, what had I lost? The treatment, or so it seemed to me, was without fuss and as genuine as it was free. Nonetheless, some refused and either returned home or continued in agony. It was their choice. We chatted a while longer exchanging Camino stories until my turn came, then I hobbled over with a boot and sock in one hand, presenting a foot into the lap of the waiting Wolf. After a very brief and informal introduction he proceeded to ask me questions about my journey. *Where is the pain*? He asked. I pointed to the sore part of my foot. He grasped it tightly holding it with both hands. Silence, except for the sound of people talking after sharing the experience of a long walk in the hot sun. Then, after five minutes, someone came over and said that he was wanted on the telephone.

Wolf apologized and said he would be back soon to finish the job. I waited and considered myself fortunate to be here in this tranquil hostel offering free medical treatment. He appeared and clasped my foot with both hands once more. There we remained for about another ten minutes. I became aware that my foot was getting warmer by the minute until it felt very hot in the area where there had been pain and soreness. I felt optimistic. Finally, Wolf let go of my foot and was confident that I could complete my journey without further pain or fuss. I put my sock and boot back on and walked away feeling great.

Some said that Wolf had the sign of stigmata on the palms of his hand but I never noticed.

Later, after a meal and a shower, I went into my dormitory and crashed out on my bunk bed. I hoped to make an early start. Before getting to sleep I heard voices in the darkness speak in German, French, Italian and, more often of course, in Spanish. These are the usual languages heard on the Camino though English as a second language was also quite popular for people who did not know each other's language.

Finally I went to sleep dreaming different dreams until at 5.00am I awoke. I lay still for five minutes amongst the snores and first stirrings of life in a room shared with a dozen or so other people, contemplating the previous day's events. I felt full of energy. Something had changed. There was no pain and I felt very confident, in fact far more confident than I had for a long time.

I decided to get up and walk. So I got dressed, picked up my fine wooden stick placed underneath the bed, put on my rucksack and marched out of the building about ten minutes later. I walked to Leon where I had breakfast and carried on. I walked and walked. I walked for thirty- three miles that day and nearly as far the day after that.

It was much the same story for the rest of the walk, which was completed about a week earlier than if I had continued at the same pace I had walked for the first half of the Camino.

Thank you, Wolf.

Incarcerated on Mars

After a few months spent teaching English in Saudi Arabia it was time to return to England - but what a time it was, I can tell you.

My hotel suite was well furnished and it was something of a novelty to look outside through the steel bars of my lounge window at the dusty red and orange world beyond. What with the ever-present dust storms, periodic flash floods, and of occasionally being locked inside the hotel, I felt as if I was incarcerated on Mars.

Many evenings I would sit and chat with other teachers about our predicament. Each workday morning we would meet up in the hotel foyer to catch a private taxi into work – which was a well-made shack not far from the Yemeni border. There we would teach English to young Saudi employees most of whom were keen to learn.

I was fortunate to have a great class of sixteen lads who responded well to ideas, games, and anything else which furthered their learning experience. Other teachers had different experiences, but there was one thing we all shared in common. We all worked for whom we considered to be the worst employer. Experience suggested that this was nothing more than a boot camp that paid well. Each teacher – there were about a dozen of us – had his moment of persecution when something he did or said was considered unacceptable.

For example, in addition to the five hours teaching a day we had to fill in a report on each student which assessed their strengths and weaknesses in terms of whether a student was passionate enough or caring enough or professional enough. This report contained many more categories and all had a numerical value and took more time to complete than the teaching hours allocated.

I rarely had more than ten minutes to prepare my teaching lessons for the day such was the workload and demands of management for administrative slavery. But this was not enough. Each form and punctuation therein must be 100% perfect; if a comma or full stop was considered out of place, or not visible, a teacher would be reprimanded.

Any noticeable dissent would mean the likelihood of incurring some verbal show of hostility, and some felt the threat, even the actuality of violence, was never far away.

On one occasion teachers were informed that their weekly evaluation sheets returns were not good enough, yet for what reason was never fully explained. How perverse is that? I found this style of management incomprehensible.

Every week we therefore had to not only teach and fill in IT forms galore but create a test paper of the highest professional standards for employees to answer as best they could. The results were then evaluated and noted on a variety of forms, which were logged onto a computer and sent to management. Deadlines were a constant feature and woe betide you if evaluation sheets, test papers, or any other piece of information arrived later than expected.

For the end of semester exams teachers were again asked to set and assess exam papers, as if we had nothing better to do. There is far more to this story, and for me, it ended after a break back home and reports of security risks in the region when the Americans closed their embassies. In fact over half the teachers never returned to their teaching jobs after a two week obligatory break. One teacher has written online about being denied leave to go to the funeral of his father. He resigned shortly after this and now teaches elsewhere.

NO SACRED OXEN

It was 2.00am at Dubai airport. I was on my way home and had to wait fifteen hours for a flight to London so I found a suitable looking bar and, after ordering a beer, sat down in front of a large television screen. Within a few minutes a cold glass of Stella Artois was carefully placed on the table in front of me. It was very refreshing and had the effect of washing away the previous months' experience. It cost £9 and, although not quite a pint in my estimation, it was worth every last drop. This was a cause for the celebration of freedom. Having escaped from the equivalent of an incarceration on Mars, I felt I had earned the right to be completely ripped-off. I paid the bill and ordered another beer. And another. And another. The end.

What Churchill's early life means to me.

Let the Fortune of the House Stand on the Faithful Dispensation of the Gifts of God. Harrow School Motto.

In reading about the early life of Winston Churchill in his autobiography, *My Early Life*, I was struck by how accessible it was to get to know him. Winston writes of his time as a child and schoolboy and the story continues into young adulthood and time as a soldier and journalist until, finally, he enters parliament representing the Tory Party. This is the point of departure and those who want to learn more about the life and career of Winston the politician and world statesman will have to look elsewhere. Yet in this autobiography there are tales of the unexpected which reveal something of the quality and character of the man. Several stories spring to mind and I will mention them here because few others appear to have done so. Until recently, I had assumed that Winston was an atheist or agnostic, but that is an assumption and not a fact. It seems to me that many have overlooked the inner or essential quality and character of Winston Churchill, not paying due regard to his revealing autobiography.

Many years previously, however, I read a much-praised biography of him by Roy Jenkins. Despite the reams of facts and well-researched anecdotes, it has transpired that I remained largely ignorant of what motivated the real character of the man who is considered by many to be one the world's greatest leaders.

As a schoolboy at Harrow, Winston did not enjoy learning Greek or Latin and questioned the logic of placing too much emphasis on the importance of a Classical education which he did not always consider relevant. Attitudes in early life appear very conservative with regards to *alterations to the Prayer Book or Marriage Service* and describes any changes as *grievous*, so there can be little doubt what he would have said about the controversial policies introduced by the present incumbent of Number 10, Downing Street. My guess is Winston would have been uncharacteristically speechless.

Further on, in a chapter entitled, *Education at Bangalore*, Winston writes about the sons of a privileged elite and ventures the opinion that a university education should only be available for those students who are in Winston's words, *thirsty for knowledge and have proved their worth in factory or field.* He may have had in mind something like the adaptation of Evelyn Waugh's novel, *Brideshead Revisited.* Without a hunger for knowledge a brilliant education can be wasted on those who see their time at university as more a rite of passage than an educational opportunity.

For Winston Churchill an education at Harrow public school nourished an ambition to join the British army for which he sat repeated exams in order to be accepted for a career as an Officer at the Royal Military Academy, Sandhurst. What his early life means to me is mainly to be found in the chapter, *Education in Bangalore.* Here he writes clearly and concisely, and I presume honestly, about his religious thoughts and views. It is to these candid, and yet for most part unreported views that I will shortly turn.

Winston's education in Bangalore was undertaken while waiting for a military posting and would mean cavalry action in Afghanistan. He later wrote articles about his military adventures although the first newspaper article he wrote was as an observer in The Cuban War of Independence, which appeared in *The Graphic* in 1895. It was through journalism that Winston sought and secured financial independence considered vital in forging a successful career in parliament. Winston's passion for writing continued - as did a growing reputation for unsurpassed rhetorical skills - winning a Nobel Prize for literature decades later in 1953 for, *The Second World War* and

NO SACRED OXEN

A History of the English-Speaking Peoples. In Bangalore, he spent much of his time reading in order to satisfy a newly found hunger for knowledge. An enquiring mind drove Winston to want to know more about ethics and religion. He read more of the respected authors of his time including Gibbon's, *The Decline and Fall of the Roman Empire* and, Winwood Reade's, *The Martyrdom of Man.*

Winston is shocked to find views challenging his traditional Christian based education at Harrow. He writes:

For a time I was indignant at having been told so many untruths, as I then regarded them, by the schoolmasters and clergy who had guided my youth... . As it was I passed through a violent and aggressive anti-religious phase which, had it lasted, might easily have made me a nuisance. My poise was restored during the next few years by frequent contact with danger.

Further on in this candid and acclaimed autobiography Winston writes about his escape from a Boer prison camp:

I realized with awful force that no exercise of my own feeble wit and strength could save me from my enemies, and that without the assistance of a High Power which interferes in the eternal sequence of cause and effects more often than we are always prone to admit, I could never succeed. I prayed long and earnestly for help and guidance.

Until reading this autobiography I had assumed that Winston Churchill was an agnostic or an atheist.

Roy Jenkins may have written about the faith of Winston Churchill but I do not recall reading it. If Jenkins did write about Churchill's prayers to a *High Power* I have either overlooked it or was not persuaded of the significance in shaping the character and conscience of the man. However, I think the latter is more likely. It is my view that Roy Jenkins, as the archetypal left liberal, would not have been interested in attributing any form of success or achievement to the crucial life threatening moments Winston Churchill spent in prayer. I doubt whether Jenkins would have given much credence to the idea that Churchill's character and conscience were shaped by thoughts on theism. However, the theistic opinions of Churchill are as clear as a full moon in a cloudless night sky. Winston Churchill, who eloquently expresses a belief in God, became instrumental in saving the world from oppression and tyranny. Thank God for that.

Footnote

I returned to reading the biography by Roy Jenkins and discovered that he did indeed write about Sir Winston Churchill's South African experience evading capture and so on. What is telling is that whereas Churchill writes in his biography of his faith and attributes the act of prayer to a *High Power* as instrumental in his destiny, Jenkins - who must have read Churchill's autobiography - explains this epiphany away as nothing more than, "luck".

Obviously, Roy Jenkins knew better than Sir Winston Churchill himself about the life he had lived and the reasons for a stratospheric rise and influence in this world. According to Jenkins it was all based upon *luck*. My guess is that Jenkins was thinking rather more about himself than the subject of his biography, Sir Winston Churchill.

Swings and Roundabouts

In the amusement parks of early 1970's London I gained the impression that the witch's hat and roundabout had already begun to be phased out.

Too dangerous, I suspect. Not in my estimation but in the minds of those who, years later, would make a good living from an industry often described as *health and safety* which in effect tells people how they should live and what type of amusements are best enjoyed by children.

What remained in our local park were a small slide, a climbing frame, a few swings - there was usually one deliberately swung over the top bar of the frame several times hanging abandoned in a mangled knot of chains - and a red and yellow plastic seesaw.

One day in the summer of '73 I spent a couple of hours on a seesaw enjoying the sunshine with a friend. Like most playground amusements cooperation was encouraged because unless another took part nothing much happened. Even for a piece of apparatus like a slide children often had to wait their turn and this meant learning another form of cooperative behaviour. Outdoor boyhood pursuits were often instructive.

But my friend and I were past the age of childhood. At fourteen, approaching fifteen, we no longer found the amusement of using a slide that interesting. Not as interesting as a swing which effortlessly carried the weight of most people and the momentum and movement back and forth seemed to encourage an exchange of thoughts and views. Some would chat for hours on the swings unconcerned or unaware of the fading light.

NO SACRED OXEN

Returning to the seesaw, we sat for about an hour or so. I was on one end and Dit Dat, on the other - so named because his elder brother had got tired of hearing, "I want dit, and I want dat". I noticed Dit's arms were almost as brown as his vest, and we sat happily perched on the seesaw chatting about our latest thoughts on this and that. A recently released Alice Cooper album was a likely topic. We both liked the band's music and Dit listened to little else at the time. His newly acquired habit was to carry around with him a battered cassette recorder blaring out *halo of flies* or some other Alice Cooper song. This afternoon, however, the cassette recorder was curiously absent from his side. I presumed the batteries had run out.

The seesaw moved up and down slowly according to the rhythm of conversation. We were not in a hurry, but as we were talking and sitting astride our respective ends of the seesaw - sometimes lifted up in the air, sometimes hitting the ground - we became aware of a gang of youths who had quietly walked into the park. They were now making some noise and seemed intent on causing trouble.

There were six of them and about sixteen or seventeen years of age, several years older than us so we were not really considered a threat but this was not immediately apparent. Responding to this change of situation I asked Dit:

"What shall we do?"

It was a good question, I thought, but his answer was better. Not for its wisdom but for the fact that he seemed to be completely unfazed by the turn of events. In other words, Dit was phlegmatic about the whole thing. He took it all in his stride and answered me just as the seesaw was taking him into the air and me down to earth.

"Let's stay here. We'll be okay".

NO SACRED OXEN

I believed him. If Dit wasn't worried why should I be? We had known each other since early childhood and had often been out together scrumping apples or gooseberries. We went to the same Primary School and then to the same Comprehensive. We played in the same woods nearby. And, we played in the same football team. We knew each other fairly well. It wasn't always so. When we first met we fought on The Green near the stream. He bit my ear so I pulled a large chunk of hair clean out from the top of his head. But all this was forgotten in the boyhood escapades that followed.

Meanwhile, in the park, the gang kicked anything that didn't move and had now focused their attention on the perimeter fence. It was about to be attacked by what I imagined were devoted wearers of Dr. Martens boots. I turned round on the seesaw and saw that the gang was now kicking, shaking and pulling the high fence.

I lost my nerve, *"Shall we run for it Dit?"*, I asked.

"No, it will be fine." He replied.

And there we remained until we thought it better to go to them rather than wait for them to come to us. Instinctive reactions took over I suppose. So seeing no better option and frankly bored with a scene which demanded our attention we dismounted from our seats and walked over to the leader of the gang. He appeared less aggressive and more concerned with conducting events than in wasting his energy on the destruction of inanimate objects.

We asked him why they were here and where were they from?

Reasonable questions which were met with a not unreasonable answer:

NO SACRED OXEN

"We are from Ponders End. We have taken your park. Tell your friends."

So we did. We left the park and told everyone.

Not long afterwards a car pulled up and four youths got out, closely followed by another car of youngsters delighted to find that a worthy enemy was in town. Streams of younger children followed in their wake. In the space of an hour the whole place had been transformed. Even the weather had changed and was now cloudy, overcast and threatening to rain.

The sky changed for the lads from Ponders End too. Hordes of disaffected youth had turned up emerging from council estates near and far to save the park from the worst Ponders End could throw at us. The Ponders End mob bolted and ran down a nearby alley and into some fields, closely followed by fifty or sixty boys aged from nine to eighteen who chased after them. Dit and myself looked on wondering whether to join in, which we did for a while, but gave up as this story evolved into something resembling a long distance cross-country race.

We never saw the Ponders End crew again although we subsequently heard some stories about their demise. Life was a bit of a seesaw in those days.

The big blue lorry

There once was a child,
A kindle he did make,
One night alone,
A fire he was to light.

His parents returned,
Just in time,
But the fire in the boy's heart,
Had been extinguished forever.

Wherever there was love,
He chose hell.

What could be done?
The neighbours tried,
And the Police did call.

But with a big blue lorry
The lonely boy banged
The bedroom wall
In desperation.

This sorry tale of woe,
Is only overcome by love,
Which knows of its Divine source.

Except for His love,
What else can sustain thee?

A day trip to Muscat

On a bright spring morning a coach departs from a college in Rustaq. On board are twenty-five Omani students, young men and women, about twenty years old, and a teacher of English. Travelling down the main highway, they pass arid sandstone hills and fort-like houses.

I chat with the boys at the front who are keen to learn more about me. As we talk it is easy to hear feminine voices in the background. The girls are happy at the back of the coach. My lessons with my usual class have unexpectedly been rearranged as I have been asked to accompany a group of slightly older students on a day trip to Muscat. As is usually the case in Oman it is a sunny morning.

The coach journey normally takes about ninety minutes depending on traffic. This time, however, we alight onto a recently built motorway providing not only an alternative faster route to Muscat but unexpected views on the jagged crested mountains silhouetted in front of a clear blue sky.

The girls are laughing as we arrive into Muscat and our first visit of the day, an interactive museum of Omani heritage and culture. Inside students mill around and learn more on geology and ancient ways of life up to the present day. But this feels too much like education for a leisurely day out and we are soon back on the coach and off to a nearby souk to do some shopping.

The souk in Muttrah - a part of the old and the new Muscat - is a bazaar experience. Narrow alleyways honeycomb an area of hundreds of small shops selling everything from gold, frankincense and myrrh to antiques, pashminas, perfume, and exotic incense burners, all under a single roof. It is said that this labyrinth of passages thronged with white-robed Omanis and a plethora of visitors from Europe and elsewhere is the most popular tourist destination in Oman. As in numerous other markets around the world haggling for the best price is often worthwhile and expected; an art which was expertly demonstrated by the students when helping me in my purchase of a particular item. Students were, by now, hungry and it was decided by common assent to find somewhere to eat lunch.

On the way out of the souk it is possible to see a giant incense burner atop a hill on the edge of Muttrah Harbour. At least this is one explanation for in all my visits I never saw the evidence of any incense being burnt or what would be the sign of characteristic fragrant smoke billowing out from such an unusual and prominent building. The so-called incense burner is as likely to be an alien spaceship if looks are the measure of things. Whatever its function the incense burner adds a certain spectacle to what is a magnificent harbour view particularly the vista of the final part of the Al Hajar Mountains, which divides a low coastal plain from a high desert plateau. After the meal with the students I find out that our next coach stop is to a fairground a short distance away and that is when life can be a bit of a roller coaster. I sat in the middle flanked on either side by hijab clad Omani students who laughed nervously in anticipation for the fairground ride to begin. Beside me girls sat in quiet and happy expectation and further along the row I noticed more smiling faces accompanied by what sounded like hysterical laughter. For the moment the machine remained stationary.

From the high vantage point of the carriage most of the other attractions of the amusement park, including a Roller Coaster and Dodgems, were visible. I could see some young Omani boys wandering around the funfair. The boys appeared disappointed that I had chosen to spend my time with the girls in their separate search for amusement. Out of the darkening blue there was a mechanical noise and the machine lurched into action. Huge pistons bore the weight of about a dozen people and a thick steel bar held each person tightly inside their seat. It was necessary to stop anyone falling out and I checked that my steel bar was locked into place. We were then thrust forward and descended much like carriages fixed onto a Big Wheel revolving from top to bottom and round again following a circular motion of 360 degrees. This particular ride was not as high but this was not its attraction. Depending on speed and movement, whether the circular motion was forward or backwards, the carriage occasionally turned with passengers hanging upside down for a minute or two. I became aware of being part of an anachronistic scene and glanced either side and thought that life is full of surprises. There were some screams from one or two girls further along the row as we hung suspended in mid-air. It was dusk as we had waited for the machine to begin but by now it was night and fairground lights illuminated what had previously looked like a collection of isolated metal structures.

After happily alighting safely right side up and having taken the opportunity to survey much of the area, albeit from a novel position, it was time to investigate further. Some of the girls bought ice creams and chatted away until finding the bumper cars. Other girls were interested to know more about the different cultural experiences I had encountered while teaching in other countries.

I thought of the time when I was hiking on the rocky coastline of Dalian in northern China and had stumbled upon a beach crowded with young Chinese taking an unexpected national holiday and break from their work or studying. What surprised me was how awkward they looked having nothing to do with this unplanned free time.

By contrast Omani students had grown into their unexpected holiday with independent ease and as I looked at their black hijabs considered that this disguised a self- confident spirit often unappreciated by those who think that clothes maketh the man or woman.

NO SACRED OXEN

Despite the allure of other rides we remained waiting for the Bumper Cars to start. There were about a dozen electric cars now occupied by an impatient driver. Eventually someone turned on the power and away we all went. For a while the girls whizzed around finding sanctuary in ever-changing space as hunter and hunted re-enacted an ancient ritual. From time to time a maverick might interrupt the usual course of events sending one car crashing against the side of the oval track. More usually, however, most were content with avoiding being hit but this had as much to with luck as skill or the intent of the assailant. It was a lot of fun and quite different from six hours previously when I stood in front of the whiteboard introducing the active and passive by writing, *why did the chicken cross the road?* And, after identifying subject, verb, object (SVO) writing this timeless question into passive form only after having elicited student answers.

All this had happened earlier in Rustaq where barber shops abound. In Muscat, however, we had drifted away from the sights and sounds of the fairground for further refreshment at a pavement café but this time I was accompanied by male students, all wearing a hat or sometimes a *muzzah* - a type of turban - and a *dishdasha*, which completes much of the appearance of the white Omani national costume.

It was nearly midnight and although few were in a hurry to get home it would take an hour or two to arrive in Rustaq and so we boarded the waiting coach. It may have been just another hot day out in Oman but it was full of surprises and insights, which for me turned a physical journey into a memorable cultural experience.

Answers on a postcard

Why is it that abbey ruins are often far more sublime and beautiful than new modern buildings?

Could it have anything to do with what a building represents?

If one was built for the worship of God, what is the likely function of a new building today?

Chow Mein

It can take years of living in a country to find out tiny details. For instance, I had been teaching English for nearly four years when I noticed that whenever I asked for chow mein in restaurants in China, I would occasionally get a blank stare. The pronunciation expected was, chow me-an. Chow mein or chow me-an? When to use one or two syllables for mein?

Two different pronunciations appeared to be mutually exclusive. Usage might depend on the region or the education of the listener. More likely what I said was not enunciated clearly enough or was I making a meal of things? Whatever the ins and outs of pronunciation, the quality of food is a prime ingredient in Chinese culture. In China people regularly introduce themselves by enquiring:

Chi guo la ma?

This is pinyin for, "Have you eaten yet?" This informal enquiry, as another way of saying hello, emphasizes how important food is in China.

Chow mein, as everyone knows, is mainly noodles and mince beef and typically delicious. The most basic cafes charged as little as 50p or the equivalent in 2005. For me it became a staple diet especially in the evening when street vendors open up food stalls thereby providing an alternative street scene to concrete and neon. There is something very human about sitting on a plastic chair eating chow mein with chopsticks in the evening. I recommend it.

Students I taught came from prosperous middle class families in the coastal city of Ningbo. Ningbo is much smaller than Shanghai and located about one hundred miles due south of the second largest mainland city of China. Massive building projects and developments include the world's longest sea-bridge which now connects Shanghai and Ningbo. Apparently this new bridge has reduced road travel from 400 to 80 km. The longest sea-bridge prior to this connects the Japanese island Kyushu with Honshu and built by the Japanese decades beforehand.

Chinese technological accomplishments have greater significance and represent the return of China as a powerful and influential nation. Indeed for some nothing less is expected of the oldest living civilization in the world. It would not have gone unnoticed that the Chinese bridge was longer than its Japanese predecessor. I did meet Chinese who lived and worked in Japan and vice versa but it struck me that neither group felt entirely at home in each other's culture.

Team games sparked competition and student interest might be increased by a carefully chosen team name written in chalk at the top of the blackboard. Not thinking too much about it for one of my initial classes I wrote: Japan v China. More often than not about a third of the students no longer felt any animosity towards the Japanese for real or imagined wartime crimes. A further third did not know or care much about such things either. This left a final third. They were passionate about this subject and devastated if they were chosen to represent Japan in a game. Several students visibly wilted at the prospect and some stared despondently at their desk. Others simply shouted, NO!

I thought it prudent to abandon the idea and focused instead on different categories. For example, boys versus girls or, team A versus team B. The result was improved harmony in the classroom and most teachers are grateful for small mercies.

Once a week I looked forward to teaching a particularly happy class. After fulfilling the demands of the curriculum and reading exercises from a prescribed book it was time to teach students the time or, more accurately, how to tell the time in English. Most students already had a good grasp of this but I thought it would be beneficial for them to have some more practice. So after students had performed a ritual morning eye exercise class preparation was put into action.

The eye ritual, as I call it, involved children sitting at their desks and listening to instructions in Chinese over the tannoy system. During this short break students closed their eyes and placed the knuckles of their hands into each eye to shut out the light. There then followed some light movement or massage of fingers on closed eyelids. My impression was that this was supposed to stimulate in some way the eye. Only a few wore glasses so perhaps there was something in it but I never found out more about the health benefits or otherwise.

There are many ways to say and tell the time. On the blackboard I drew twenty clocks showing all different times. It was a big rectangular blackboard and there was ample room to show almost any time imagined. Clocks showed: twenty past six, half past two, five to three, two-thirty, ten to ten, ten-forty, twenty to ten, nine o'clock, quarter past twelve, quarter to twelve, five past twelve, and so on.

Team games engaged student interest and encouraged participation so with this in mind I divided the class into those representing Ningbo versus students representing Shanghai. Two students volunteered to be the first to take part and promptly stood in front of the blackboard. The class looked on in keen anticipation. Finding a central position from which to best conduct events, I said a time: "half past one". A student could be quicker off the mark and apply his piece of chalk to the correct time before the other was able to act or gather in the information. Though once in a while contests could be closer and more amusing.

NO SACRED OXEN

In the Chinese educational system I experienced it was not uncommon for children to be streamed according to age rather than ability so with up to a maximum of three years age difference it is possible to have a class of students aged between, say, twelve and fifteen. For a twelve year old to be in an older class suggested, to me at least, that they were quite able although they were noticeably smaller than the older students invariably found at the back of the class.

The next pairing of students stood in front of the blackboard and waited for me to say a time. The rest of the class remained seated and also waited. I noticed a girl nearby nervously glancing across at me. What was different on this occasion was the size of the two students, both of whom were by far the smallest in the class.

I announced: "Twenty-five past five." The small boys facing the board swung into action immediately with arms and bodies and legs moving in several different directions at once. Movement appeared balletic and rhythmically synchronized by leaping from the blackboard's top centre to the far right hand corner. Almost at once both boys were again staring into the face of the wrong time and wrong clock, so with an energy previously undemonstrated, they displayed in unison an agility of mind and body to sweep back and across to the left hand side looking once more for the correct time. For a moment everything was a blur as short arms whirled around in front of the blackboard with chalk clasped tightly in tiny hands. The scene resembled something from Walt Disney's, *Fantasia*. Students had become an audience at a show and the entire class was convulsed in laughter.

The girl sitting beside where I stood thought it hilarious, and so did I. After about a minute or two, the boys matched the time I had announced with the clock time drawn on the blackboard located in the centre and with increasing momentum the chalk held by one boy marked the clock, a fraction before the other, and was declared the winner. He was asked to correctly say the time identified whereupon he sat down happily basking in his victory.

My main class, however, involved teaching English to a group of about a dozen Chinese students aged from sixteen to eighteen. Their educational ambition was to study at a college or university in England. It was my purpose to guide them in this direction by making known to them not only a variety of grammatical exercises which could often be dry and laborious but to initiate some of the more enjoyable aspects of English teaching abroad which includes music or educational games.

The main class was located near the running track at the side and back of the school campus. Here I would sometimes stand on a balcony overlooking the scene and consider how many laps I would be able to run next time for this area had become something of an outdoor gym. My record was twenty-seven laps in one hour and I never managed to better it.

My preference, however, was to play table tennis whenever the opportunity arose which, in China, it often did. I rarely played table tennis before arriving in China but in a short while had discovered a natural ability at the game thereby enabling me to encounter and experience another oriental diversion.

I had never taught before except in the process of gaining a CELTA Cambridge certificate so it came as a shock to find that my first six months were spent teaching the same group of twelve students nine hours a day, everyday from 8.00am to 7.00pm. For this initial period there were no other teachers teaching this class. All preparation, all ideas, all aspects of teaching had to stretch the ability of this little group of sixteen to eighteen year old privately educated, Chinese students.

NO SACRED OXEN

Fortunately, a Chinese teacher named Andrea, sat at the back of the class ready to assist in any difficulties that might arise either in translation or organization such as social activities which all helped in improving students' performance, if not attendance.

Many people under the age of thirty in Ningbo liked to use an English name, and if they didn't, I might be asked to think of one. It was easier to remember names of students I had chosen: Paul, Steve, Mike, to mention but a few. Even the Head of the school liked the idea and so after some deliberation decided upon the name, Hannah.

From time to time I was invited into the homes of some of the students. I noticed a similar theme of large outer walls and big copper doors. Inside the house there was not quite the homeliness I expected. Everything appeared new and expensive or spick and span but something more personal seemed to be missing. This contrast between homeliness and something less so became more vivid after visiting the homes of less affluent students and their families.

Not far away, sometimes just across the road, was a small factory owned and managed by the father of one of my students. Some of the fathers owned up to ten factories. I ought to have taken more interest in what they produced but one example I can think of involved the processing of metal so that a copper wire might end up as a conductor or some type of ornament or one of the numerous copper doors facing out from many wealthy Chinese homes.

It was during the Spring Festival that the Chinese teacher in our classroom invited me to visit her grandparents. It was a long drive out into the *countryside* as Chinese describe it although from an English perspective the lack of green grass and a few solitary trees suggests something other than countryside. But countryside it is to the Chinese and can be used pejoratively by those who have grown up in cities and know little else. The word *countryside* in China implies a region where people are poor and often less well educated. Anyway a trip was duly arranged.

The town had seen better days or maybe it hadn't. My impression, however, was of a place in transition. Many Chinese cities were changing quickly. The growth rate in urbanization of the largest populated cities sometimes meant the reverse for less popular areas. A winter sun shines and shade appears framed by clearly defined lines.

The less populated towns were losing more and more young people who sought jobs and better career opportunities in the expanding cities. But this was not always the case. One town I visited was visibly bustling and thronging with young people despite its close proximity to Shanghai. The air quality, however, was not so good.

The home of Andrea's grandparents felt warm despite the cold and different from the large, expensive, well-insulated houses of well-off students. In contrast this was small and basic – no central heating - and had been lived in for decades. As Andrea translated I was offered something to eat and drink and learnt that the grandfather had fought with the Chinese army in Korea in the early 1950s. But all that remained in the past.

On arrival I noticed small stickers stuck on doors and cold walls connecting staircases from one level to the next. Each sticker displayed unreadable information and a mobile telephone number. The growth of the prostitution industry in China was apparent everywhere. The grandmother expressed annoyance with the present and lamented these changes in culture and society or at least this was the impression I gained.

Before returning back to the city I went for a walk with mother, daughter and grandmother. We did not have to go far to find a railway station and platform. It was deserted. I was not sure whether it had been abandoned and left to the ongoing process of incessant change so characteristic of so-called modern society. Amongst this bleak background I took a photograph of three generations of women standing on a deserted railway platform bonded by love.

We returned to the house and I drank a bowlful of Shaoxing wine, slept and dreamt a familiar dream.

Years later, I learnt that the poet, Samuel Taylor Coleridge, noted the lack of surprise felt in sleeping dreams. The following excerpt and first stanza, of the poem **Kubla Khan** (completed in 1797 and not published until 1816) was a work reputedly inspired by a vision within a dream.

> *In Xanadu did Kubla Khan*
> *A stately pleasure-dome decree:*
> *Where Alph, the sacred river, ran*
> *Through caverns measureless to man*
> *Down to a sunless sea.*
> *So twice five miles of fertile ground*
> *With walls and towers were girdled round:*
> *And there were gardens bright with sinuous rills,*
> *Where blossomed many an incense-bearing tree;*
> *And here were forests ancient as the hills,*
> *Enfolding sunny spots of greenery.*

Samuel Taylor Coleridge.

The Venerable Bede and what his writing means for my understanding of Irish and English history

Talk for any length of time with many an intelligent Irishman and you will soon become aware that being English is not something to celebrate. And, since many Irish men and women have lived in England for centuries and can vote in English elections it might account, in no small measure, for an English cultural disposition of muted national self-regard. Generally speaking, this is considered to be a national characteristic as humorously elucidated by Ian Hislop:

"Modest about our national pride - and inordinately proud of our national modesty".

This attitude seems preferable to jingoism. Perhaps modesty, as a national characteristic, is something to be proud of after all. Yet there seems to be a prevailing Irish view which, broadly speaking, says that national modesty is fine, but the English have a lot to be modest about as far as the impact of English history on Ireland is concerned. This opinion can, and in my experience often does, assume a morally superior position. Most people have heard of Oliver Cromwell, The Potato Famine and, Bloody Sunday. Who was the aggressor? Who was the victim? These are usually rhetorical questions.

Researching more into the subject, however, I discovered a more complex historical story. What I have recently read about is at odds with the stories I have heard which argue that the British threw the first stone. The thing is, it all depends on how far back in time you want to go.

Return to the time of the Venerable Bede who wrote about the people who lived in the British Isles and Ireland prior to 700 AD and a different picture emerges.

For instance, some of the earliest written accounts of Irish and English history inform that the Irish - sometimes historically referred to as Scoti - were the protagonists and instigators of violence against the native Britons.

According to Bede it is revealed that the Irish joined forces with the Picts, whom they advised to settle in England instead of Ireland. If they met any resistance, the Irish promised they would assist the Picts in securing their new land. Eventually, the Irish allied with the Picts, played their part in this ongoing moral high ground debate as invaders and aggressors of the land occupied by Britons.

For illustration, Bede writes:

"...the Pictish race from Scythia sailed out into the ocean in a few warships and were carried by the wind beyond the furthest bounds of Britain, reaching Ireland and landing on its northern shores. There they found the Irish race and asked permission to settle among them but their request was refused.

The Irish answered that the island would not hold them both; 'but', said they, 'we can give you some good advice as to what to do. We know of another island not far from our own, in an easterly direction. If you will go there, you can make a settlement for yourselves; but if any one resists you, make use of our help."

And further on Bede writes about the subsequent plight of Britons:

"...the people were utterly ignorant of the practice of warfare. For instance, they were rapidly reduced to a state of terror and misery by two extremely fierce races from over the waters, the Irish from the west and the Picts from the north; and this lasted many years."

NO SACRED OXEN

"As a result of these invasions, the Britons sent messengers to Rome bearing letters with tearful appeals for aid, promising to be their subjects for ever, if only they would drive away their threatening foes."

In playground language, who started it? In metaphorical terms, who threw the first stone? In law, it is often asked when assessing the validity of a claim for criminal injuries, who threw the first punch? In each and every case the answer is: The Irish did.

My maternal grandfather's family line is from Ireland - he was known as, Paddy - so this is not about racism or settling scores or anything like it. I have always got on well with most Irish people which usually includes a couple of Irish friends and hope this will continue. This time, however, the moral high ground, from my perspective, is unoccupied.

Main reference:

Bede: Ecclesiastical History of the English People. Penguin Classics.

Voyage and Return

Men's faults do seldom to themselves appear.
Shakespeare.

At various times in my life I have met a friend from my childhood or teenage years and we have discussed how much life has changed, but there is one instance where time seems to have stood still. One Christmas I bumped into the parents of a teenage friend who suggested that I pay them a visit over the festive season especially since they were expecting their son to stay over during this period. I had not sat in the lounge of their home for thirty years yet here I now was noticing once again that each home has its own smell. The television had changed. It was more modern and the screen was about three times the size to the one I had previously seen. There was a new carpet and very new furniture. Everyone was relaxed and I waited for some fizzy white wine. My friend grinned and enthusiastically poured the remaining contents of a bottle into my beige mug.

Apart from this not much surprised me. He had, like myself, aged but no more than anyone else, in fact, perhaps less so. What surprised me was not his physical appearance which resembled the teenager I used to know, but his mannerisms, diction and conversation. What he said and the way he said it. His voice and intonation were as I remembered. Even the way he laughed reminded me of the person I used to know. I had never experienced this before. I think I have changed but perhaps only someone who used to know me well can say by how much. We drank and reminisced on a variety of subjects and then talked about his brothers. In due course, I finished my drink and left wishing everyone a Happy Christmas.

When I arrived back home I thought more on my conversation and realized that most of the words and sentence structures had not changed either. What was said invariably contained lashings of collocations, clichés or well-worn phrases, words I had heard millions of times beforehand; it was the parlance one might expect watching *EastEnders* or *Big Brother*. I thought it unlikely that he had followed a path similar to my own. This was a path that had been challenged by numerous educational and intellectual hurdles. A path I had willingly walked upon, but considered was unfamiliar to my friend. He had taken a different route. We both shared a comprehensive school background and I think at that time his educational progress was greater than mine or at least recognized as better by those who decide these things. I was, therefore, all the more surprised by what appeared to me as intellectual stagnation.

Looking back on this now I realize that such things might be more common than first thought. On another occasion I met someone I used to know who said they were reading Harry Potter books and something by Russell Brand. This sharply contrasted with the person I once knew who found the stimulus of philosophy and poetry far more rewarding. I recall *The Republic* by Plato, or Dante's, *The Divine Comedy* placed upon a table at her home; not an incongruous picture for someone with a first class Theology degree.

Perhaps I have travelled in the opposite direction. In my formative years I used to read comics and *The Daily Mirror* but after about the age of thirty regularly began reading *The Times* newspaper. Several years after this upgrade in my everyday reading this newspaper also succumbed to the ubiquitous tabloid design so I changed to *The Telegraph,* and now things have changed again preferring, like many others, to scan news stories for free online.

But what is possibly more unusual is that I rarely watch television. For educational entertainment I enjoy travelling or reading biographical or historical books. And I prefer to travel independently and finding my own path and route to a saner world. It has taken a while and there have been more than a few distractions and mistakes along the way but it has been largely an educational path which, on balance, is better taken than not since without improved education and qualifications I would not now be able to the job I do which so far has afforded me the opportunity to teach almost anywhere in the world. The alternative would have meant conforming to the banality of English office culture, fine in my early twenties, but not so rewarding in later life particularly so in a culturally Marxist politically correct context where so-called human rights overshadows duties or responsibilities at every turn.

On reflection, I think it more advantageous to be not only as well-educated and independently minded as possible but in having an enquiring disposition which is not intimidated by a depth perspective so often found in literature outside the usual list of best selling newspapers or television shows or the most popular books. I would rather that my head was not filled with socially engineered left-liberal dogma broadcast *day in, day out* into most homes in England. I don't know for sure whether former friends have been passively culturally brainwashed, but after some discussion with them, I suspect it.

Following a Rock band from beginning to just after

I first heard about AC/DC on my doorstep. Geoff and Stuart stood there enthusing about a sixteen-year old lead guitarist from Australia whom they had seen on stage at the Marquee club the evening before. They were attempting to persuade me that it would be in my best entertainment interests to come along with them for the second and last performance.

I let them ramble on and heard more about Angus Young, his uniform and guitar playing ability, and decided that I must join them on this quest for the best ever gig. It threatened to be in London this very evening so I quickly finished my meal and put on my favourite t-shirt and jeans.

The three of us then left my parent's house and marched up the road and onto the tube alighting at Leicester Square and, after a brisk walk, arrived at the Marquee club an hour later. It was early May 1976, and AC/DC, an Australian outfit, were supporting Back Street Crawler.

The gig I attended was the result of a postponement. Back Street Crawler now featured, Geoff Whitehorn, a new lead guitarist. The previous guitarist - formerly of the revered English rock band, Free - Paul Kossoff, had died at the age of twenty-six a month or so beforehand as a result of a heroin overdose. At the time, however, I was seventeen and only vaguely aware of the tragic circumstances surrounding the headline act. For myself, and a few others in this already well-known darkly lit venue in the heart of London's Soho, it was undoubtedly the support band we had come to see. I had only a short while ago heard of the antics and theatrics involving a youth dressed in schoolboy uniform. What is more, he could play his red SG guitar like a maniac. The scene beckoned and was pregnant with anticipation. Only later would there be the necessary climax.

So there we stood, three teenagers, in a tightly packed crowd eagerly awaiting a sound from a microphone announcing a rock band featuring either an English drug addict or a deranged Australian. It was heady stuff. And, quite how Bon Scott introduced the band is lost in the mists of time, but I'm sure it did not take him too long before he was singing and strutting around the stage in blue jeans and bare chest with his bag pipes wailing:

> *"Riding down the highway,*
> *going to a show,*
> *Stop in all the by-ways*
> *Playing rock 'n' roll... ."*

And on to the chorus:

> *"I tell you folks,*
> *It's harder than it looks,*
> *It's a long way to the top,*
> *if you want to rock n roll."*

At the time, however, I wondered what type of rock band uses bagpipes on stage?

Most bands avoided them for reasons similar to those who don't like working with animals and children. Yet Bon Scott seemed to not only be able to play the bagpipes he could create a sound that matched perfectly the rock tempo of the music. Amazing. I was impressed.

AC/DC had arrived. True to instant legend Angus Young really was young and not only did he wear schoolboy uniform but he played the guitar better than a maniac.

From thereon in my friends and I followed AC/DC on their formative days in London watching them play a few feet in front of us at places like the *Red Cow* in Hammersmith. It was there that we found the band to be friendlier than most and so in the months that followed we got to know them all quite well, though some more than others.

During the long hot summer of 1976 the band played a residency at the Marquee, appearing every Monday evening for six weeks. After the gig, a friend and myself, invariably caught a night bus and then walked the rest of the way back home arriving at about 4.00am, emerging three hours later to leave for work.

That summer, AC/DC played the Lyceum in The Strand in London where, on a stage compered by John Peel, I came third wearing a t-shirt with an imprint of a suit and tie on the front which was given to me by the band and paraded for all to see above a pair of shorts in the *best dressed schoolboy/schoolgirl competition*. The crowd had a lot of fun watching their peers attempt an Angus Young persona.

They also did another one off gig at the Marquee club. During the set, and in between numbers, the band asked me which song I wanted them to play next?

I was taken aback. I shouted out, *Can I sit next to you girl* (the b-side of the single , *It's a long way to the top, if you want to rock 'n' roll)* which they rarely played on stage but you would never have known it for the sound was as tight as ever and I was chuffed to bits.

Geoff, Stuart, Dave (the wheels) and myself followed AC/DC over the length and breadth of England seeing them play in pubs and cinemas, in clubs and at universities. Cambridge University was particularly memorable with a fantastic lively crowd to match the energy of the band. After the gig we met Mark Evans, the bassist, in the pub for a few drinks.

NO SACRED OXEN

The last occasion I saw AC/DC was when they played at the Hammersmith Odeon. Before the band appeared on stage, I got talking with the girl in front of me and asked her whether I could sit next to her? *Yes*, she replied.

Window shopping

Recently, while teaching somewhere in the Middle East, I went out and bought a McDonald's quarter pounder with fries and a coke.

Before that I went window-shopping and so bought nothing, but in the shopping Mall I saw the following:

Shop 1: Women's dresses
Shop 2: Women's dresses
Shop 3: Women's dresses
Shop 4: Women's dresses
Shop 5: Women's dresses
Shop 6: Women's dresses
Shop 7: Women's dresses

And so on and so on until I saw shops catering for female fashion; a retailer offering cosmetics, an expensive jewellers, and a shop displaying children's dresses.

Walking further on, I noticed several more shops selling women's handbags and women's shoes.

I then came across scores more shops selling women's dresses. The women, however, waiting for the shops to open, wore nothing but black from top to toe. It appeared that at home they all intended to dress differently.

Secular Myths

For a long time I have accepted secular and conventional wisdom on the Catholic Church. I had thought that the Catholic Church was rich. People told me so. I believed it.

I had thought there might be something in the claim that the Catholic Church had a lot of money in the bank. So it is often asked how could an extremely rich Vatican truly represent the poor and marginalized of this world?

This is a very good question until I found time to read more into the subject. What I found surprised me.

In the acclaimed book, *Sacred Causes,* by Michael Burleigh there are numerous stories that shed light into the prevailing secular darkness. For instance it is revealed that:

"During the first world war, Pope Benedict XV gave away his own fortune and then the Holy See's ordinary revenue to repatriate prisoners of war and civilian refugees, so that by 1922 the Vatican treasury amounted to the lire equivalent of £10,000."

Now this breaks a few secular myths, does it not?

I wonder how many people were hitherto as uninformed as I had been on this issue? The irreligious create these secular myths whilst ignoring an *inconvenient truth*, which is not the fallacy of global warming, but a heartwarming story of a Catholic Church made practically bankrupt in its effort to alleviate the suffering of the survivors in the aftermath of WW1 and the Russian Revolution.

During the 1930s it is well-known that many on the political Left in Britain were sympathetic to communist ideals and allowed themselves to be taken in by Soviet propaganda. The Soviet Union was believed to be a just egalitarian society promising peace, land and bread. This was another secular myth believed by a fair proportion of the British Labour Party at that time. However, in many regions of Russia the truth was very different for millions of Christians who were persecuted by an increasingly hostile atheistic Soviet state.

Stop the Cavalry

"Doth it not show vilely in me to desire small beer"
Henry IV (Shakespeare)

I went on a brewery tour today. Much talk about yeast and hops and barley and most of it homegrown. My first impressions were mindful and guarded.

Introductions suggested that this was going to be a tour of outstanding politically correct proportions. Best keep my thoughts to myself. This seems to be part of the cultural landscape of England today imposed from above. Is there no escape from this national brainwashing?

This reminds me of an exchange of views I had with a friend on the subject of political correctness. His view was and is that despite the possibility that some might abuse language for their own purposes, political correctness was mainly a good thing since it meant that certain pejorative words could no longer be used against people from a so-called ethnic minority and that this had to be a good thing.

I agreed, but even in this regard there is the matter of immigration and successful assimilation.

I think the point has been made elsewhere that pejorative words hastened effective assimilation as those who were considered in some way other became as one with their host country largely by adopting the same customs and habits.

In England, for example, many councils have used taxpayers' money to pay for educational material to be made available in a variety of ethnic languages, thus removing the incentive for someone to learn the host language. On visiting a local library I picked up a leaflet printed in about a dozen different languages.

The strange thing is my job involves travelling round the world teaching English to people from other countries. English learning is in demand. It is the lingua franca of the time, but don't tell left-wing inclined English councils.

The real scandal is that after over a decade of mass immigration and thousands of new laws it is the indigenous people of Britain who are forced by politically correct government to assimilate to the demands of a multicultural society rather than the other way round.

This is the real scandal. By ignoring the truth of the matter politicians and even our journalists betray their country and its people. Meanwhile, back in the brewery expectations were happily confounded.

After the tour concluded we sat down in the bar and listened attentively to the tour guide as he wound down from his task. Some brews were ordered and these were passed around on a clean, beige wooden table to taste.

By this time the tour guide was chatting with a middle-aged couple noticeable by their accents as coming from the Midlands region of England. I went up to the bar to enquire about the cost of a unique whisky on display and promptly returned to my seat.

As the conversation involving the Midlands couple and the guide was coming to an end, I overheard, *"...and that is why we have lost our country."*

Well blow me down! From being the personification of political correctness the tour guide had suddenly become a human being, and a patriotic one at that. I very nearly fell off my perch. I agree mate, I said.

Divine conscience

U p until reading Evelyn Waugh's biography on the Jesuit Priest, Edmund Campion – who was hanged, drawn, and quartered, for attending to the souls of men – I was of the opinion that the English Tudor Queen, Elizabeth 1st , was the best of English women and well deserved her glorious reputation as an intelligent woman of conscience and a great Queen and leader of her people.

Indeed, in a BBC poll in 2002, Elizabeth 1st came seventh in a list of the 100 'Greatest Britons'. However, my opinion has now shifted. The sky has changed. The window of history seems very different this morning.

Elizabeth 1st took an oath of allegiance, which had not yet been superseded by the issue of the Prayer Book or acts enforcing its use. In other words, Elizabeth 1st affirmed her responsibility to the spiritual needs of a Catholic country in a ceremony which was conducted by a Catholic Bishop not yet deposed.

The following is of historical, religious and political interest because Elizabeth 1st broke her oath in that under her reign as Queen of England hundreds of Catholics were persecuted, tortured and put to death. These were the following oaths:

Bishop: *Will you grant and keep, and by your oath confirm... the Laws, Customs and Franchises granted to the clergy by the glorious King St. Edward, your predecessor?*

Queen: *I grant and promise to observe them.*

NO SACRED OXEN

Bishop: Will you keep peace and godly agreement entirely according to your power, both to God, to the Holy Church, and to the people?

Queen: I will keep it.

Bishop: We beseech you… to preserve unto us and to the Churches committed to our charge all Canonical privileges and due Law and Justice; to protect and defend us, as every good King in his Kingdom ought to be Protector and Defender of the Bishops and Churches under their government.

Queen: With a willing and devout heart, I promise…that I will preserve and maintain to you and the Churches committed to your charge all Canonical privileges, etc."

Three hundred and twelve English Catholics were martyred during the reign of Elizabeth 1ˢᵗ. The stripping of the altars continued. After many centuries of Catholic religious tradition first documented by the Venerable Bede in the 7ᵗʰ century, a popular way of life was suddenly considered unlawful. Catholics were persecuted.

Elizabeth clearly had not observed the customs and laws of her *glorious predecessors.*

People were fined for attending Mass. For not attending the new Protestant service, fines were introduced. A repeated 'offender', someone who either attended a Mass in his or her home (or did not attend a Protestant Church service) would risk being sent to prison. Some prisons were worse than others. And, some deaths were worse than others.

In 1581, Edmund Campion was martyred. He died for his country and its Catholic religious tradition.

NO SACRED OXEN

In 1603, Queen Elizabeth was at the end of her reign and sat on the floor refusing to eat or sleep. She was plagued by nightmares and refused to go to bed explaining:

"If you were in the habit of seeing such things in your bed, as I do in mine, you would not persuade me to go there."

A letter to those who support the EU

"Membership of the Common Market will forfeit our insular or commonwealth wide character." — *Winston Churchill, Cabinet Memorandum 29, dated November 1953.*

"We are with Europe but not of it; we are linked but not compromised. We are associated but not absorbed. If Britain must choose between Europe and the open sea, she must always choose the open sea." — *Winston Churchill, House of Commons on May 11, 1953.*

As we can see, one of the greatest men in British history would have been against the EU as the supranational interest we know today. Winston would have argued with all his might against the likes of Cameron, Miliband and Clegg. Political pygmies they undoubtedly are. As for the views of Tory EU supporters, they ought to hang their heads in shame at their betrayal of a nation that once stood head and shoulders above any other, not because the people were better than others but because the people and great men stood against tyranny whenever it threatened others.

That tyranny once existed in the forms of Napoleon and Hitler. Britain matched them with Nelson, Wellington, and Churchill. And beat them. Britain secured a freedom for Europe and the world. Inspired by the parliamentary campaign of William Wilberforce Britain did much to free slaves who were still traded in America, Africa and the Middle East.

Empowered by public opinion the British Navy was able to not only command the high seas but to enforce freedom. No one else did or could. No one. But you will be unlikely to hear much about this at any British comprehensive school. Why?

NO SACRED OXEN

Because of the latest tyranny: cultural Marxism. Useful idiots abound in their desire for peace at any price and in finding personal satisfaction in parading a public view of claiming the moral high ground not caring a damn for either the people or their country. Sir Winston Churchill would be speechless at the culpability of the latest batch of British political leaders who have soiled the memory of great men and a once great nation.

The Najdorf: a personal view

Five hundred million people play chess worldwide.

I began playing chess from about ten years of age. Since then I have played as and when until playing regularly online. And, during the past few years, have played chess on a fairly regular basis. Until a few years ago the only chess literature I had read was on games played by the former world champion, Bobby Fischer. I think he was arguably the all-time best chess player and have noticed how often it is that his opponents made errors. This is not to say that Fischer won because of others' mistakes, far from it. It suggests that Fischer was so good that players doubted their ability to beat him. I imagine this is what happens when playing a champion or genius.

It is only relatively recently that I have begun to appreciate the games of other world-renowned chess players such as Garry Kasparov, Alexander Alekhine and, Jose Raul Capablanca. *Chess Fundamentals,* written by Capablanca, is an essential book for anyone who seeks to build a foundation for future chess play and knowledge. It is timeless instruction from one of the world's best natural chess players. Jose Capablanca is renowned for having been a chess genius and for a natural ability in understanding instinctively the demands of any chess position. Others may have successfully copied his style of play but for those who are starting out and want a deeper and more fundamental understanding of chess it is often best to begin with reading the words of an original.

Capablanca is known as a brilliant positional player. His thoughts on strategy are lucid and insightful for most chess players hoping to improve their game. Both Bobby Fischer and Anatoly Karpov, said they were not only inspired by Capablanca but that they learnt a lot from the style of his positional play.

NO SACRED OXEN

By studying the games of Capablanca it can be instructive in finding thematic positions or patterns of play suggestive of whether a player should be looking for the best move or whether just a good move will do. In chess competitions time is a factor for evaluating positions. It is easier and takes less time to find a good move rather than the *best move,* which ordinarily is harder to find. Chess is typically subjective and relative to the demands of the position.

However as most good chess players are only too well aware there are objective principles in chess. For more detail on this some study is required of Wilhelm Steinitz who was a prolific writer and the first to establish positional principles in guiding a player's search for the optimum or most suitable moves. Likewise, Aaron Nimzowitsch, another influential writer who introduced a system of playing chess. The Soviets dominated the world of top-level chess for many decades thereafter debated and discussed basic chess principles amongst themselves in their closed society. The American GM, Bobby Fischer, in the 1950s had to learn Russian in order to read some authors who had established a modern consensus on chess principles. Such principles can be discarded in favour of a subjective approach but few know when it is wise to do so.

Evaluating chess positions, however, is as much about tactics and calculating combinations as it is about strategy, planning or positional play and some say that this is the reason why the tactical wizardry of Alexander Alekhine finally eclipsed the positional genius of Cuba's, Jose Raul Capablanca in the World Chess Championship which took place in Buenos Aires in 1927.

The Queen's Gambit was then a fashionable line for opening with the White pieces and for many it still is especially for those who prefer queen's pawn positions which are generally regarded as safer than king's pawn games. For instance, moving the pawn from **d2** to **d4** rather than **e2** to **e4**. (Bold type hereon in represents moves by the player of White pieces).

Please also note that the algebraic notation method is preferred and has replaced descriptive notation, which would once have referred to the aforementioned moves as: **PQ2** to **PQ4** or, for the alternative king's pawn move, **PK2** to **PK4**.

My best result was a win against IM Tony Ashby in a twelve player simultaneous display in 1985. I played with Black the *King's Indian Defence (KID)*, which was effective against White's aggressive **d4, c4, e4** attack. This particular system of defence, however, no longer works as well as it once did for me. It could well be that there is more in the *KID* position to study and that is what is required to improve results but now I prefer to play the, *Bogo-Indian, Nimzo-Indian* or *Queen's Indian Defence*, against Queen's pawn openings.

In the 1990s I played Harriet Hunt who became a very highly rated player and women's GM. I played her when she was still quite young at Cowley Chess club which was then, and maybe still is, an exceptional club for its nurturing of out of the ordinary young chess talent. The games I played against Harriet were instructive as many lost chess games often are, but I was pleased to have had the experience of playing someone as good at chess as she undoubtedly was even in her formative chess playing years. What struck me was not only how adept she was in her positional play but how skilfully she used her knights deftly undoing any position I thought secure.

Knights are often used in defensive positions but their modest power can be maximized further up the board for offensive play in closed or static positions such as when the board is packed with pieces and pawns and there is little room for manoeuvre. This is an example of when a knight can be of more value than a bishop. In open or more dynamic positions, however, the reverse is usually true. A bishop can then exert an enormous influence on the game by virtue of the range of squares it can control, albeit of either dark or lights squares. Conversely, a knight becomes weaker the fewer pieces remain on the board and the more open the position.

Two knights cannot checkmate an opposing lone king. A fact I was unaware of prior to reading the aforementioned book by Capablanca and helped in gaining a draw against a fairly decent player who had not yet evaluated this particular feature.

Another example, when another draw was achieved against the odds by understanding the position as outlined by Capablanca's writing, was when playing an opponent online and who was attempting to queen a pawn with the aid of a rook and king. My rook and king acted in concert to prevent this happening. Only through teamwork on either side of the pawn was it prevented from continuing on its journey of transformation.

How to evaluate a position?

Generally speaking, it is helpful to have some kind of guide or template to apply when evaluating a chess position. At least I have found such knowledge helpful. This advice might be of use to a beginner since I am not an IM or GM and not qualified to advise anyone on improving their chess except, perhaps, the novice.

With this in mind the following questions are reckoned to be helpful in evaluating the merits of a position and in deciding on which move might be a suitable candidate for further thought:

NO SACRED OXEN

1. *Who controls the centre of the board?*

The centre is the high ground of chess and crucial. If you control the centre think of as similar to being 1-0 up at half-time in a game of football.

2. *What is your plan?*

What side of the board do you want to attack? If possible disguise intentions and timing of an attack.

3. *What are your initial thoughts?*

Intuition is worth considering but so are any concealed factors and this takes longer to evaluate. What to do? Decide whether a position is critical or stable, open or closed, dynamic or static, before deciding whether to spend more time on it. In any chess game there will usually be several moments for thinking about concealed factors such as whether the dynamics of the game is about to shift from closed to open? If a position is closed or static it is often a characteristic feature of chessboard cramped with pieces and pawns and very few open lines available for rooks or bishops. This position invariably favours knights. Knights are able to jump over pawns and pieces and so are unlike other pieces that are restricted by clutter. Open positions favour bishops and rooks. Unrestricted by a closed position such pieces exert more control on more open squares thereby increasing their power and influence on the result of a game.

4. *Does the move chosen act in concert and harmony with other pieces?*

Quick piece development and teamwork usually wins the initiative and chess games. The initiative is when one player has greater possibilities for attack.

5. *What is the opponent's plan and how are you going to exploit his weaknesses?*

This will involve further evaluation of the position and a keen sense of timing. When will an attack have most chance of success? It is advantageous to attack with tempo. Tempo can be gained by attacking a stronger piece with a lesser piece.

6. *Prophylaxis?*

What are you going to do about threats made to your pieces or position? It is possible to anticipate what the other player will do and when their threat is greater than yours it is wise to consider defensive options or a prophylactic move. Sometimes this will mean simplifying a position by exchanging pieces. Other times it will mean stopping the opponent from playing a move he had wanted to play. For example, **a3** or **h3** are moves often played by the player of the White pieces so as to thwart an attack featuring a bishop or knight played to b4 or g4.

7. *Sacrifice?*

Sometimes it is necessary to sacrifice a pawn to improve positional prospects in the centre or elsewhere. A piece sacrifice is more common when seeking an effective attack on the enemy king or queen.

8. *What square is important to contest or control?*

Often a central square but can be any square on the board. Whether the square is light or dark is also of consideration especially when evaluating bishop moves.

9. *Where is the space?*

Quick and early development of pawns and pieces is mainly advantageous if not only because the power of a piece is usually increased the more squares it controls.

10. *Patience*

A position is advantageous if it is flexible and as adaptable to changing circumstances as possible. But a chess player will also often require patience when playing defensive minded or positional players who tend to win games by exploiting errors than they do in creative or attacking play. In chess aggressive play can and does have it rewards as it can induce errors in the play of the defending position. But patience is also required as some defences are better than others. In some cases moves played will be to frustrate the opponent rather than do anything creative to win the game. In such circumstances I have found it advantageous to sit tight and play *a cat and mouse game* and not to try to force the position. To do so might undo whatever advantages have been made and within a few moves might see a won or drawn game lost.

Once the process of evaluating a position becomes second nature I think it more likely than not that results will improve for anyone new to chess and wants to progress.

The Najdorf is my favourite Sicilian defence primarily because it is flexible and adaptable and consequently easier to create an attack from the confines of defence.

The Najdorf is one many types of Sicilian defence which begin with 1...c5 as a response to White's King's pawn opening, 1 **e4**.

Particularly instructive in playing the Najdorf is book by Gambit publications entitled: *Mastering the Najdorf,* by Arizmendi & Moreno – Spanish IM and GM respectively.

The Sicilian defence usually begins when playing Black against White opening with:

1 e4
2 Nf3
3 d4

The Najdorf is only recognisable as different from any other Sicilian Defence employed against King's pawn attacks when Black plays:

5... a6

This unassuming or so-called *quiet move* signals the beginning of the *Najdorf* as opposed to any other Sicilian system and is popular because it is supremely flexible and responsive to a variety of closed or open positions.

The Najdorf will mainly appeal to those whose inclination is to attack rather than defend. This often means counterattacking and hopefully with decisive effect in positions not only considered open and dynamic but also *sharp*. Sharp, is an adjective used to describe a position which is more tactical than strategic, meaning that decisive moves may depend more on calculating combinations rather than positional factors alone.

Any blunder made in a sharp tactical game can be decisive.

The Najdorf is played by the player with Black pieces and is named after the Argentinian GM, Miguel Najdorf, who popularized this system in the 1940s. It offers flexibility and a huge range of creative possibilities with regards to tactics and strategy. In view of this it is often considered more exciting than other defensive options available.

The crucial point in playing the Najdorf is to recognise not only when to play a move but what to play especially after evaluating the merits of White's sixth move. Depending on the pattern of play Black must consider whether to move the pawn to:

6...e5 or, e6?

There are a number of options but it is thought thematic to consider the following responses. For example, when White plays an aggressive bishop move or a pawn to h3:

6 Bg5
or
6 Bc4
or
6 h3

Then, the player with Black pieces should respond with moving a pawn to:

6...e6

In nearly all other instances Black should play e5. There is one notable exception, however. If White plays:

6 Bd3

This is an unorthodox but natural move. From what I can gather the best response by Black is to play:

6 Nc6

In summary, and to clarify the position outlined for this discussion, the following notation refers to the first six moves involving Black's response to White's, King's pawn opening which characterize the Sicilian Najdorf:

1 **e4**	c5
2 **Nf3**	d6
3 **d4**	cxd4
4 **Nxd4**	Nf6
5 **Nc3**	a6

Black's fifth move, a6, completes the initial combination of moves identified as the Najdorf, rather than any other Sicilian system.

What White plays next for the sixth move determines whether Black plays: e5, e6 or Nc6. If White plays anything other than **Bg5, Bc4, h3** (or **Bd3**) Black plays 6...e5. Armed with knowledge of what to play for Black's sixth move: e5 or e6 or Nc6, a player can begin playing with a perhaps a little more confidence than might otherwise be the case.

Incidentally, when playing the Najdorf, d5 is considered a weak square and is typically protected by placing a bishop on e6 at some early stage in the development. However, circumstances might suggest that the bishop would be better deployed on b7, while covering the same weak square on d5. Either way d5 requires attention, and as I understand it, is the only inherent weakness in the system.

Recommended reading

Arizmendi & Moreno: *Mastering the Najdorf*
Isaac Lipnitsky: *Questions of Modern Chess Theory*
Edmonds & Eidinow: *Bobby Fischer Goes To War*
Bobby Fischer: *my 60 memorable games*

NO SACRED OXEN

Jose Raul Capablanca: *Chess Fundamentals*
Van der Sterren: *Chess Fundamental Openings*
Boris Gulko & Dr. Joel R. Sneed: *Lessons with a Grandmaster*
Martin Weteschnik: *Understanding Chess Tactics*

Peace in our time

"The EU is godless. But then it is unthinkable that the EU could build a common European house while ignoring Europe's identity. Europe is a historical, cultural and moral identity before it is a geographic, economic or political reality. It is an identity built on a set of values which Christianity played a part in moulding." Pope Benedict XVI

It is reported that despite having a few billion quid tucked away the Ministry of Defence is quietly putting itself and the UK out of business. Never mind that the political class expect the military to go anywhere in the world in order to enhance a global and compassionate image. Never mind that the British Army was once considered the best professional outfit in the world. Never mind all this. All the while there are plans afoot to increase the size and presence of EU forces especially in the Mediterranean region. Is it possible that the expansion and spending on EU forces is a plan that will eclipse and eventually replace funding for British forces? In my estimation this is what lies behind the latest betrayal of British sovereignty by the political class. And while we are on the subject will the EU honour a British NO vote in the forthcoming referendum?

This case does not rest on what happened to Eire and others. The political machinations of the EU – which has a finger in almost every political pie in the UK – has made it so that many influential people are financially rewarded for being adherents of the EU and its political ambitions for becoming a European Federal State. It is not just about economics which was the first big lie sold to the British public during the referendum of nearly forty years ago; it is about political affiliation to a European Federal State.

Monetary union was always going to be one way of achieving this which has been resisted more by luck than political judgement by the UK left liberal political elite. The funny thing is despite an EU cultural emphasis placed on the values of equality and egalitarianism, all things are far from equal. I would be amazed, but of course very happy indeed, if the British people said NO to the EU while the EU and political elite in the UK accepted this decision. And I hope they do accept it because it would strengthen a weak democratic system. And it really does not matter how much more powerful than Eire the UK is because many people in the UK have a vested interest in remaining tied to the EU gravy train. EU subsidies on thousands of schemes make this a reality from Cornwall to London to Yorkshire. Don't forget that all these subsidies are borrowing from Peter to pay Paul. The UK taxpayer pays the EU a massive membership subsidy every year. This money is returned in the form of crumbs which fall from the EU table to the delight of those who are willing to accept, what is, I suggest, no better than political bribery. Think of Wind farms, for example. Who makes them? Who has shares in them? Who profits from them? And, what damn good do they do except blight the landscape? Why does all this concern me? I believe this reveals a political process that has undermined national sovereignty and the democratic parliamentary process. British governments of every hue have betrayed the people they pretend to represent. They say they want change, but only change that suits their common purpose. What is their common purpose?

An EU Federal State based upon supranational cultural Marxist principles. If you want this, vote to remain in the EU. If not, vote OUT. Better still, vote for a Party that wants OUT, full stop.

"Democracy Matters"

"What is the city but the people?" Shakespeare.

I was born in London and have lived and worked in England for over four decades. In spring 2005 I took a job teaching intermediate English in China. Since then much of my time has been spent teaching abroad. What follows is a record of correspondence as I attempt to register my eligibility to vote in the General Election before leaving to take up another teaching post, which is expected to last about ten months. Advice and information provided is given by those who are responsible for the administrative process of electoral democracy in north London, where I grew up, and are here shown in bold and my response in italics:

Your father has recently bought (sic) **in a letter regarding your request to vote by proxy but unfortunately we are able** (sic) **to grant this request as you are not registered. You will need to send the form/liase** (sic) **with — ———————— as you will need to register as an Overseas Elector with them as they will need to check their registers to ensure you were registered – unfortunately, we cannot register you on the — ———— Register as you need to register with the council where you were last registered to vote.**

So I decided to make further enquiries. The reply follows:

As my colleague has explained, you must register as an overseas elector with the borough where you were last registered to vote. As this was in ——————————, you must contact the office covering that area. The fact that you have

lived in ------------------ for so many years does not count I'm afraid. This is according to the regulations of the Representation of People Act that we have to comply with. The Electoral Commission website explains the process in full. The web address is --- .

In view of the above information I contacted the **About My Vote** website. Their reply follows:

Thank you for your email, and I'm sorry you've had problems using About My Vote. Could you tell me a bit more about the problem you've experienced? When you say you cannot access the website any further than the local authority search page, what happens? What are you clicking on? Do you get an error message?

Sorry to come back to you with more questions, but I hope that if you let me have this information I'll be able to find out why this is happening. I would suggest that you contact your previous borough before sending the application forms just to make sure that they have a previous registration for you but that is up to you. I am sorry we cannot be of more assistance to you. Democracy matters. Please consider the environment before printing this email.

My response here concludes this discussion. I am, however, still waiting for a reply:

Thanks for your latest email. Pity there is no email address available for me to reply to you directly. I can now access the site and download the form but I do not presently have the facility available to print off this form. Even if I did would I really have to fill in a form and send it from China? And, to whom do I send it?

I have been making enquiries about voting for nearly two years. How difficult must it be? It seems that I am running out of time. After all of the enquiries and all of the form filling and all of the arrangements made I doubt whether I can vote in the forthcoming election.

Finally, it may be noted that during this correspondence I contacted the office of my local MP who were helpful in advising upon an idea of presenting a *proxy letter* as mentioned in the second line of the first piece of correspondence received. However, despite initial optimism I am still unable to vote in a UK election.

"Democracy matters", they say. Does it indeed?

* According to a recent newspaper article in the Daily Telegraph, one million Britons live in Spain, yet only 18,000 of these potential voters registered a vote in the last General Election.

Constantinople

There are several games that are used for teaching purposes in the classroom that are usually popular with students. The first of these games is called, Constantinople. The main purpose of the game is to increase the vocabulary of students with regards to different categories of interest such as verbs or nouns, or adjectives, comparatives and, superlatives. The latter group is useful after completing some class study of adjectives and how they can change in form when being used as comparatives or superlatives. For example:

clever, cleverer, cleverest

The main appeal of this game, however, is that it involves everyone. A student representing one of four teams stands at the front of the classroom with their own colour marker pen in hand and ready to write words according to letters beginning with each letter in the ancient city name of: C O N S T A N T I N O P L E.

Other students remain seated and call out their answers to assist with completing the activity. The team that does this quickest with least mistakes or spelling errors is declared the winner.

This game has been introduced to students in China, Thailand, Oman and Saudi Arabia and in all these places it has absorbed the attention of most students who often deserve some fun after a more formal format of teaching. This is one good reason why Constantinople is one of the most popular games in the classroom in my teaching experience. The game is introduced to students in the following fashion:

NO SACRED OXEN

	Team A	Team B	Team C	Team D
C				
O				
N				
S				
T				
A				
N				
T				
I				
N				
O				
P				
L				
E				

After drawing lines on the whiteboard students are informed of a few rules to enable the game to run as smoothly as possible. Students are advised not to repeat words and to avoid copying. Through trial and error they learn that copying others ideas not only minimizes their learning but that what is copied is not necessarily correct.

Depending on the level of ability words chosen are from five to nine letters to fit a particular category deemed best suited to a particular learning experience. The above example and illustration would therefore proceed in three stages when completing a lesson on comparatives: Adjectives, Comparatives and, Superlatives.

In most other instances in playing Constantinople there would be one stage only such as when writing types of nouns or verbs or whatever category is considered relevant at that time to enhance and further understanding.

After the game drills involving each team are encouraged to elicit correct pronunciation of each word written on the whiteboard by a particular team. In the case of Arab learners of English the letters b and p are sometimes confused and more attention is required on this particular aspect of pronunciation.

Another class activity more recently introduced is based upon dictation to further writing and listening skills. After the exercise students are invited to read out what they have written. Errors in pronunciation are occasionally corrected at the time of speaking but more usually after the oral exercise is completed when more time is available for corrections and drills.

The second stage to the dictation activity begins when students turn over their paper and write down specific words read out aloud by myself. Students with most words spelt correctly stand at a whiteboard for a final bevy of words once again said aloud by myself. This activity I found to be very popular in Saudi Arabia and should the occasion demand it I will consider using it again.

Picking daisies with Darwin

"Men became scientific because they expected law in nature, and they expected law in nature because they believed in a lawgiver." C.S. Lewis.

If a dinosaur fossil were to be found in Swanage today it would presumably be of great scientific interest, greater than, say, finding other types of fossils such as a brachiopod or a trilobite.

Therefore it seems strange that the first scientifically discovered dinosaur fossil - found in Sussex, England, in 1824 – was of little or no scientific interest to Charles Darwin who wrote **The Origin of Species** published some thirty-five years later.

Given Darwin's acclaimed polemic in *Natural Selection* would it not have been of supreme interest for the findings of recent discoveries of dinosaur fossils to be investigated? Especially since they were so conveniently close to hand?

Human blood groups differ from those in Primates. Darwin said there was little difference between chimpanzees and homo sapiens. Whether this difference is of interest in evolutionary terms is uncertain, but is worth mentioning nonetheless.

Belief in a creator God is as believable today as it was yesterday or in the Victorian world of Darwin. A universe created by a transcendent divine mind or consciousness is far more plausible than a 10 to the 139th power of random chance.

As I see it a concept of God is the best explanation for the origin of the universe. Is there a better one? The universe had a beginning; most agree with the latest scientific evidence to assert this claim. But was the beginning by chance or design? This is where faith or opinions part.

If it is claimed that we are here by chance then the chances of the world existing (as we know it) are estimated by the astrophysicist, Dr. Hugh Ross, to be:

"...less than one chance in 10 to the 139th power (ten thousand trillion, trillion, trillion, trillion, trillion, trillion, trillion, trillion, trillion, trillion, trillion.) exists that even one such planet would occur anywhere in the universe."

Many appear to be dismissive of the idea of a transcendent divine consciousness creating the universe – yet open to an explanation based on an astronomical figure achieved through random chance – conveniently putting to one side that such a view demands a far greater leap of faith than they seem to admit or acknowledge.

It has been said that some evolutionary changes require a whole mass of interdependent changes, which have on occasion resulted in inexplicable leaps of evolution such as the formation of the eye. Some Darwinist's say that *every single fossil is transitional.* How do they know? Would intermediate features constitute a gradation according to Darwinian theory?

Other evolutionists might say that perfection cannot be achieved yet it is towards this particular ideal that Darwin gazes yet remains unsure whether perfection can ever be found in the natural world? He did not need to look far? Did the renowned Botanist never look at a Daisy? Is it not perfection? How can it be improved?

Darwin's depressive state of mind, he no longer enjoyed the arts, listening to music or reading poetry, began in middle age – which contrasts sharply with his extraordinary good fortune through independent wealth, position, and opportunity - was not in my view entirely based on the death of his daughter whom he loved. But he had ten children and three died; a fact not uncommon to Victorians who were arguably made of stronger stuff in those days. After reading of how Darwin lost interest in the arts and music it seems to me that it is entirely possible that his conscience was pricked by what had been written and the political implications thereof. For example:

"Darwin's book is very important and serves me as a basis in natural science for the class struggle in history."

Karl Marx.

A concept of God

Is God a girl? Or, is God an Old man with a white beard?

Richard Dawkins thinks God is the latter. This viewpoint reminds me of a quote I recently noticed about dogmatists by G.K. Chesterton:

"Everyone cannot help but be a dogmatist, and there are two kinds: 'the conscious dogmatists and the unconscious dogmatists'. But the latter are by far the most dogmatic."

Some think of God as transcendent and outside of space and time, a spirit or divine consciousness. How do you see God?

Life Diving Championship: A leap of Faith

Free will is a complex subject expanding exponentially in complexity when considering alternative or opposing views such as, Determinism. So the idea of a Life Diving Championship appealed to me and is used here to further an understanding not only of my place in the world compared with others but what might happen thereafter.

In most important diving competitions competitors take a leap into the unknown. They expect to land safely and most do but the main thing is to enter the water with aplomb.

Marks depend on the quality of the dive but how is one to judge a dive? One dive might be better than another is one answer but is this not a subjective assessment?

To the experienced eye one dive is noticeably better than another especially so if each dive depends upon a degree of difficulty decided beforehand by the judges. For example, when Gary Hunt won the Cliff Diving Championship in Oman he did so with a degree of difficulty of 6.3 performing twists and turns and three somersaults: a triple quad.

A perfect dive would mean that there would be no chance of anyone beating him because he had chosen the highest degree of difficulty. Although the dive was outstandingly good, it was not perfect; yet he won the competition because of the degree of difficulty was at the highest level. Had a competitor chosen a far easier dive and did this with perfection it would not win because the degree of difficulty would be low. Marks are awarded according to the difficulty in making the dive and the more points are available for a more difficult dive because there is more that can go wrong and success is more difficult to achieve. And so it is with life.

NO SACRED OXEN

In the Life Diving Championship the current PM of Great Britain stands proudly from a great height and surveys all that he commands below. But his degree of difficulty is low.

The PM is fortunate in that his parents were wealthy, loving and intelligent and that he had the best education in the world money can buy. Considering all this becoming PM is an achievement but hardly a great surprise. In the Life Diving Competition scheme of things his degree of difficulty would be a modest 3.0; demanding no more than a few twists and turns and quite a bit of spin. The dive might be perfection itself but a final score would be multiplied by 3.0.

By contrast, consider the man who becomes a teacher after a childhood experience involving parental ignorance and neglect. There would be no shortage of food or materials but from the age of five parents were often absent in the evening. The child felt abandoned. His state schooling was second rate compared with what is experienced in most Public Schools and any exam success went unrewarded academically except for a new blue bike bought by his father.

Back to the Life Diving Competition, unlike the PM, the man with a difficult childhood has a degree of difficulty approximately equivalent to the one freely chosen by the world diving champion, Gary Hunt. This is a 6.3 and to accomplish such a dive requires an enormous leap of faith and fortitude. Only after several attempts is the dive successfully made. It is not perfect by any means yet a triple quad is accomplished. A score for the final dive is awarded and multiplied by the degree of difficulty, in this case, 6.3.

In the Life Diving Competition the current PM finishes joint fourth. Of course, this result would not apply to the former wartime PM and Nobel Prize winner, Sir Winston Churchill, but he is an exception to the rule. The rule is that the degree of

NO SACRED OXEN

difficulty is a more accurate reflection of any achievement and not the result of the achievement itself.

With all this in mind I have devised a points system featuring the great and the good and, the not so good. How do they match up in a Life Diving Competition according to the vision of Dante's, *Divine Comedy*?

Competitors	Degree of difficulty	Achievement	
Karl Marx	4.0	4	= 16
Adolf Hitler	5.5	0	= 5.5
Joseph Stalin	5.5	0	= 5.5
Sir Winston Churchill	4.9	10	= 49
Charles Darwin	3.5	7	= 25
William Shakespeare	4.5	8	= 36
John Keats	6.2	7	= 43
David Cameron	3.0	6	= 18
Me	6.0	3	= 18

Review

Perhaps predictably, Sir Winston Churchill wins the Life Diving Championship, with Keats in second place and Shakespeare, third. Keats, like Shakespeare before him, had the benefit of a classic Grammar School education which was arguably superior to that taught in many schools today.

However, unlike Shakespeare, the childhood of Keats bore the brunt of tragedy in the form of family death including both parents which in one form or another affected the future of Keats not least because he had to spend time caring for those who were dying which included his mother. What Keats achieved in such difficult circumstances is outstanding and a triumph of the imagination.

I do not agree with Darwin's theory of Natural Selection preferring an explanation of micro-adaptation instead of a theory that has convinced most scientific opinion.

Nevertheless, the world remains impressed by Darwinism and it appears to have not done as much as harm as the doctrines espoused by the likes of Karl Marx. But the biggest surprise in my estimation is to find that my achievement in life is on par with that of David Cameron in which case there is hope for us all.

Points	Judgement
0 to 16	= Hell
17 to 40	= Purgatory
40 +	= Paradise

Conclusion

Despite being a better man than Hitler or Stalin, Karl Marx has gone straight to Hell. David Cameron and I are likely to spend time in purgatory, as are Shakespeare and Darwin. Winston Churchill, however, is in Paradise, where he belongs. As is Keats.

Is our destiny freely chosen?

I suspect that what we call *Free will* is tempered and affected by circumstances experienced in formative years. And, that any honest appraisal or divine judgement would take these significant factors into account when evaluating the consequences of error or sin.

*For those still living, estimations of achievement are of course subject to change, and may go down as well as up.

No Sacred Oxen

Xenophanes of Colophon once claimed that, *if oxen were able to imagine gods, those gods would be in the image of oxen*. This is to say that if Man imagines God it would be a God made in his image. Hence, or so the argument goes, anthropomorphism; God is the creation of Man.

This brand of Atheism, once argued by Ludwig Feuerbach, is said to have influenced the thinking of Karl Marx and Friedrich Nietzsche. Richard Dawkins, who has expressed a strident atheism, may also have had something to say about anthropomorphism but, then again, does he not write about the *selfish gene*? Is it possible for genes to be selfish? If not then the issue of anthropomorphism appears to be of wider concern. The variety of Deities represented in Hinduism, which range from cows to elephants, suggest no apparent anthropomorphism in Hinduism; although these minor gods are said to be symbolic of the unchanging reality of one God, Brahman.

Nonetheless, if Xenophanes was wrong about anthropomorphism – sacred Oxen exist in the religion of Hinduism - does this mean that the atheism of Feuerbach, and others is wrong? If so, there might well be some ramifications for atheistic thinking today.

Chess Themes

An alternative method in evaluating a position is to identify the main chess themes. This thought occurred to me while watching game seven of the recent world chess championship match between Anand and Carlsen. The new world chess champion, Magnus Carlsen, played with the black pieces. This particular game ended in a draw but what was of immediate interest was move, 19... a5.

Magnus Carlsen thought for about fifteen minutes before making this move. The question was why this move was chosen when commentators had dismissed it in favour of, say, placing a knight on, d6? I had thought it preferable for Carlsen to challenge on an open h file by placing a rook on h8, but what was the reason behind Carlsen's idea of move 19... a5?

Most agreed that a5 was an attempt to gain space but in what way would it be easier to find such a move? Would it be possible to choose which theme was a priority or most appropriate to the position?

If it was possible to correctly identify a theme the position might be easier to evaluate and find the move that works.

I decided to do this when playing games online and have found it helpful in using this system which relies on judgement in deciding which theme is not only appropriate but a priority in any given moment of the game. This streamlines the choices available for candidate moves and so assists in the simplifying the decision making process.

Think of a clock numbered one to twelve and for each hour identify a theme as featured below:

1 *Positional planning*

2 *Tactics*

3 *Threats*

4 *Prophylaxis*

5 *Development*

6 *King safety*

7 *Is the position open or closed?*

8 *Space*

9 *Open lines and weak or strong squares*

10 *Flexibility*

11 Exchanges *(leading to simplification)*

12 Sacrifice *(for example, a pawn for an improved central position?)*

And most importantly…

13 Central control = initiative *(centre of clock)*

It is for the player to decide which theme is most important in any given position although the centre is often the best place to start. Five main themes are considered to be priorities in assessing and evaluating any given position. The chosen theme provides a context thereby making it easier for a player to find suitable candidate moves which are shown in the summary as those guided by; intuition, prophylaxis, central control, and sometimes, even crazy ideas. It was while playing too many games online simultaneously, however, that I became aware of some flaws in my technique, which after analysis, needed to be addressed in order to improve results. What I found was that I had relied far too much on intuition instead of making the necessary calculations. It is crucial, therefore, to anticipate what an opponent can do which means calculating the relative merits of combinations. With this in mind a player who makes the initial effort to calculate combinations will be in a preferable position to gain maximum advantage from their intuition.

Summary

Themes

1. Positional concerns

2. Tactics

3. Threats

4. Prophylaxis

5. Central control

Candidate moves

Evaluate accordingly:

1. Intuition

2. Prophylaxis

3. Central control

4. Crazy idea

5. Does it work?

(Calculate combinations and evaluate what the opponent can do).

Freedom

While out walking in Cordoba in southern Spain, I saw a statue of the Roman senator and philosopher, Seneca.

He is noted to have said:

"He who is brave is FREE."

Of course, what Seneca ought to have said is:

He who is brave and never despairs is FREE.

The Miner's son

This is a story of rebellion and England's descent into Cultural Marxism. Nearly five hundred years ago England's present day destiny was shaped according to events that happened inside and outside of the country. This is as true today as it was then. In 1517, Martin Luther, an Augustinian Monk decided to instigate a rebellion against the leadership of the Roman Catholic Church denying Papal supremacy. In 2017 another rebellion is brewing for it is planned that a referendum on the EU will take place. It promises to be as groundbreaking a decision as the decision to change from being a Catholic nation to a Protestant one. Once again national sovereignty is at stake, the difference this time around is that the issue is said to be secular and political. Or so it seems.

It is said that in the early 1500s and prior to the Rebellion and ensuing Reformation the English Catholic faith was in *rude health* providing not only spiritual succour but in addition attended to the pastoral needs of the poor and marginalized who could often be seen living outside the grounds of monasteries the length and breadth of England. For the common Man there was very little reason to change from one traditional Christian perspective to the subjective interpretation of Martin Luther. Eamon Duffy, an expert on the English Reformation, sheds light on a period of history hitherto subject to incessant and influential Protestant propaganda. It is argued by Duffy that:

"Pre-Reformation Catholicism was a deeply popular religion practiced by all sections of society, whether noble or peasant".

Throughout England the Protestant inspired destruction of monasteries, libraries and churches, led to religious persecution and the migration of the poor to towns and cities where they would beg for what was once freely and generously given. Christian England was turned upside down by reforming zealots whose main concerns were power and authority and had found in Martin Luther a catalyst for the realization of these ambitions.

The overall political aim of the newly-formed Protestant movement was to discredit the Catholic Church in order to legitimize the need for an independent nationalistic non-conformist church. This meant the destruction of deep- rooted ways of life. Moreover, the Pope was publicly condemned and demonized. Luther wrote in a letter:

"I am at a loss to know whether the Pope be antichrist or his apostle." Only ten days earlier, however, Luther wrote to the Pope in more polite and humble terms: *"It was never my intention to revolt from the Holy Apostolic Chair."*

King Henry VIII, whom Luther called an "impudent liar", had his own marital reasons to want English independence from Rome. It was during this time of transformation that a King became a tyrant murdering two of his wives, yet people still defend Henry for they see him as fighting for English independence against a corrupt continental influence. This is too much of an indulgence.

Rome was keen to reform from within. Indeed, the humanist Christian scholar Erasmus hoped for such an outcome and eventually tried to persuade Luther that this was a more suitable approach.

Luther was not persuaded and decided to go his own way with a personal interpretation of scripture thus usurping a thousand years of church teaching and doctrinal church councils. The consequences for medieval society and culture would be devastating.

In his formative years Luther once felt that he was in grave danger and prayed: *"Help, St. Anna, I will become a Monk"*. He described this occurrence in a letter to his father referring to this plea as a *'forced vow'*. He entered a monastery in 1505, aged 21 and later became an Augustinian Monk. The appeal to St. Anna is explained by her being the patron saint of miners and that Luther's father was a miner. St Anna is the Mother of the Virgin Mary. Now a Monk, Luther applied himself to *a rage of tasks* (unusual collocation intended) including a study of philosophy and teaching and biblical study. This eventually resulted in his conclusion of Justification by faith:

"Be a sinner and sin on bravely, but have stronger faith and rejoice in Christ, who is the victor of sin, death, and the world."

Luther did not think that sin was a barrier to salvation for faith alone was good enough. He continues:

"To you it ought to be sufficient that you acknowledge the Lamb that takes away the sins of the world, the sin cannot tear you away from him, even though you commit adultery a hundred times a day and commit as many murders."

This thinking appears to be in error for contained within the Lord's Prayer it is said: *Forgive us our trespasses (sins).* It must be asked why trespasses matter when, according to Luther, faith alone is deemed sufficient for personal salvation.

An additional point is, did not Jesus forgive the woman accused of adultery (John 8: 1-30) by using inference to expose the hidden sins of her accusers? He did, and her sins were forgiven, with a proviso – *sin no more.*

Luther's theology might be more easily understood by picturing the following saying: *the grit in the oyster makes the pearl.* As an allegory, Luther's, Justification by Faith, is presented thus; the grit (sin) in the oyster (faith) becomes a pearl (salvation). This refers to a positive outcome arising from difficult experience and must have been attractive to a man as fond of independent biblical research as Luther undoubtedly was. Yet it still seems an error to welcome sin in order to create a pearl - even if this invitation is figurative - since the vital missing ingredient in the allegory is genuine contrition as practised in prayer. It is in asking for forgiveness that a pearl is created; not simply through (the experience of) sin and (justification of) faith, which is a grave error in my judgement.

Contrary to Catholic theology Luther believed in Predestination. A doctrine that espouses the view that whatever happens depends on the will of God and there is little one can do about it except choose to have faith in Christ. For instance, *"The commands of God show us what we ought to do, not what we can do."* Said, Luther. Such opinion could be argued to justify almost any action. Indeed, in the region where Luther preached, anarchy, violence and civil war broke out which was only successfully quelled through harsh temporal means.

There are many quotes from which to draw a picture of the type of man Luther had become but whatever man it was it bears little resemblance to the man of God he was supposed to be. In his last sermon in 1546 Luther said:
"But since the devil's bride, Reason, that pretty whore, comes in and thinks she's wise, and what she says, what she thinks, is from the Holy Spirit, who can help us, then?"

Luther is said to have considered free will *a fiction,* which from my perspective suggests an abdication of moral responsibility. Luther encouraged people to sin as long as it was justified by faith. The doctrine of Predestination claims that there is no morality except by faith alone but is not this belief deeply flawed? Is not conscience the way most people begin to distinguish right from wrong?

Temptation can and does foil moral action but without conscience moral behaviour would be a far more difficult prospect than it already is. Right conduct is the key to faith. Conscience shines a light on our actions so that we can see the moral worth of them. Free will means we are free in knowing whether such a path leads to heaven or hell. Luther, wittingly or unwittingly, overlooked that faith in God demands right conduct.

Salvation is not solely about Justification by faith and holding a theistic world-view but includes Man's moral behavior and the consequences of his actions. This is as fundamental to an evaluation of moral choices as when Eve decided to pick an apple from the tree of knowledge when explicitly told not to do so. Thus is the story of Man and his temptation to sin. However, this is not the way Luther appeared to interpret this profound biblical event for he disregarded its import for reasons only he could know.

In a predestined world moral ambiguity reigns. For instance, if someone commits a crime why bother to try him if it can be successfully argued that he was somehow predetermined to act in the way he did? Moral responsibility is inherent in an understanding of free will. To argue the contrary, that a person is not responsible for his actions, is to advance towards the philosophy and theology of Luther who did not believe in free will.

As time has passed an atheistic outlook might find appeal in a Determinist explanation. The main difference between someone who believes in Predestination and Determinism is that the former believes in God and it is God who is the cause. A Determinist, will usually rely on environmental factors or causes attributed to nurture which are said to influence behaviour or the decision making process.

This seems fine for explaining reasons for choices not subject to moral or ethical concerns. A point recognized and emphasized by the world-renowned philosopher, Immanuel Kant (1724–1804), in his writing of the *Categorical Imperative* in which he placed primacy upon free will with regard to making moral or ethical choices.

From a process of subjective interpretation of scripture to rebellion and reformation intellectual pride grew until the Schism between churches brought about a new state religion in England; Anglicanism. Religious upheaval was experienced prior to and through the turmoil of the English Civil War and resulted in changes of faith from centuries old traditional Catholicism to Anglicanism which is seen by some today as being more concerned with left-liberal secular humanist causes than salvation through the life, death and resurrection of Jesus Christ.

On the continent the French Revolution inspired secular idealism in European governments but especially so in a newly independent America where the separation of church and state was written into the Constitution. The French Revolution, an anti-clerical cultural rebellion was inspired by a whole range of influential French intellectuals and thinkers such as Voltaire and the atheistic humanist, Jean Jacques Rousseau, whose antipathetic views on private property single him as preceding the political thoughts of later left-wing intellectuals. The French Revolution introduced to the world a *Declaration of the Rights of Man* emphasizing individual liberty and equality and eclipsing traditional views on religion and morality but what this new system of human rights led to was state induced tyranny.

Many atrocities were committed in the name of Reason which itself became a cult for worship. Christopher Booker elucidates in his magnum opus, *The Seven Basic Plots:*

"The idea of a transcendent God was to be replaced by a new Supreme Being, the Goddess of Reason: a glorified projection of the power of the human consciousness."

NO SACRED OXEN

While a revolutionary and a more radical form of humanism swept across France, trade and technology grew and improved, as did Man's inventiveness, inquisitiveness and exploration of the world. Science - by a process of experiment and observation - became an effective method of acquiring knowledge. Substantial progress has been made in medicine, transport and material improvements in living standards. However, moral or ethical concerns remain largely outside the scope of Science.

Many humanists today would advocate not only the primacy of reason and an atheistic world-view but in employing the methods of science to investigate all aspects of the human condition – but reason without conscience is insufficient to evaluate moral questions and can lead to Scientism.

The poet Samuel Coleridge warned in his *Marginalia* that:

*"Reason and Conscience which give all the loveliness and
dignity not only to Man, but to the shape of Man – that
deprived of these and retaining his understanding would be the
most loathsome and hateful of all the animals."*

Humanism in its modern form is no longer the preserve of literary culture and classical studies as it once was for Erasmus. Humanism now espouses scientism and atheism and it is possible to trace the origins of this way of thinking back to that time of Rebellion when a man named Luther decided that he knew best.

Much later, Karl Marx, became convinced of his own rhetoric and interpreted the world according to what he once described as a *scientific dialectic*. Whether the philosophy of Marx was scientific or not, it was certainly atheistic and despite the despotic appeal of Marxism and the economic ineptitude of those who practise it, has continued to have a baleful cultural influence on university campuses and intellectual or academic thinking in the West.

Cultural Marxism is a branch of Communism emphasizing cultural rather than an economic worldview of atheistic materialism. The adoption of cultural Marxist ideas depends on the efficacy of the indoctrination of the populace when all the institutions of the state have been infiltrated, a society not unlike contemporary Britain results.

The successful implementation of cultural Marxist ideas depends on how society responds to questions about inequality. Traditional Western Christian ideas conflict with Marxist influenced ideology because these different philosophical and economic systems do not share the same understanding of what equality means.

For the Marxist, society and culture ought to be shaped according to the greatest number of basic needs. For a democratic capitalist society, culturally Marxist influenced social engineering projects are catastrophic, for the business of a healthy capitalist society is not only to create wealth and opportunity for all but to reward talent and ability. The emphasis ought to be to incentivize rather than offer more and more state spending which robs Peter to pay Paul. One day Peter will not have enough money to pay Paul who, no longer able to live an independent life, is dependent on the state for his happiness, such as it is.

In an open free society where adults are expected to behave according to traditional values and individual conscience, personal responsibility thrives. By way of contrast, in conforming to the demands of a Socialist inclined state this essential dignity is lost.

This process of so-called egalitarianism has not only promulgated words reflecting different political priorities but a new secular puritanism as described by the insightful, Christopher Booker. He writes of politically correct adherents who believe they are:

"... acting in the name of selfless moral principles simply as a cloak for asserting their ego, and as a means to enjoy feelings of moral superiority."

The increasing erosion of national sovereignty means that it is more difficult to effectively argue against any cultural change implemented by a government who are themselves impotent when implementing an unwanted EU law. Once again this is a top down revolution except that it is not in France and it is purely secular and political.

The Catholic Church did not dispute the need for reform from within. For years the Catholic Church tolerated the biting sarcasm and criticism of Erasmus who was even offered the position of Cardinal. Erasmus had originally supported Luther but was later repelled by Luther's increasingly belligerent attitude towards the Catholic Church. Luther decried the debate for reform and preferred rebellion instead.

In a letter to Luther, Erasmus wrote the following:

"You stipulate that we should not ask for or accept anything but Holy Scripture, but you do it in such a way as to require that we permit you to be its sole interpreter, renouncing all others. Thus the victory will be yours if we allow you to be not the steward but the lord of Holy Scripture."

Despite the best efforts of Erasmus to reconcile the protagonist Luther with traditional church doctrine the result was a subjective interpretation of scripture leading to nationalism, anarchy, thousands of deaths and societal upheaval in Europe. Moreover, it can also be argued that a subjective interpretation of scripture eventually led to atheism. A look at the state of much of nominally and secular Protestant Europe today suggests as much.

In England the Welfare State provides for the needs of most without immediate means of support through the Benefits system, the National Health Service and multiple other bodies. For entertainment and social engineering many can rely upon the services of the state broadcasting company, the BBC. Those who do not pay their licence fee are fined or imprisoned. Many people are beginning to wonder whether reliance on the *Mother State* is necessarily beneficial for society and culture at large.

Moreover, left-liberal thought, has replaced the church for solutions to ethical and social problems. For example, nearly all the Catholic adoption agencies in England opposed to policies emerging from new laws centred on subjects such as homosexual adoptive parents have closed down rather than be dragged through the courts to conform with a law that is contrary to Christian beliefs which have been supplanted by an atheistic secularist agenda invoking political correctness to enforce Cultural Marxism.

The 17th century poet, John Milton, wrote of a *Paradise Lost* in one of the oldest stories known to Man. Like Eve in the Garden of Eden, the common man has eaten from the tree of knowledge, except this time the fruit is not so much forbidden but secular, humanist and scientific knowledge. People have found the taste is not everything they expected or wanted. For example, not everyone realized at the time of an initial referendum on joining the then Common Market that political promises of greater wealth and prosperity meant the loss of national sovereignty to supranational interests and the EU.

Although, by now blind, Milton's inner vision remained unimpaired, and his faith, a buttress against the wind of change; a wind that continues to blow without end through English society today.

NO SACRED OXEN

Our own good from ourselves, and from our own
Live to ourselves, though in this vast recess,
Free, and to none accountable, preferring
Hard liberty before the easy yoke
Of servile pomp. Our greatness will appear.

In reading this passage from John Milton's epic poem, *Paradise Lost*, I became aware of not only a corrupt egotism characteristic of those who so often claim the moral high ground in order to assert there own self-worth but of another dimension to the politically correct demands of Cultural Marxism which holds sway over contemporary English society. The words in the poem are meant to be those of Lucifer who justifies his rebellion from God.

All, however, is not lost. Each man retains his reason and conscience despite the ever-present effects of state conditioning and this in-built moral compass is essential to navigate through the ever-changing mist of contemporary culture. The voice within may at times be difficult to untangle from other thoughts arising but the task of doing so would be almost impossible if every moral and ethical decision was evaluated subjectively and this is the crux of the issue so far discussed.

We have already heard about the egocentricity and self-righteousness displayed by those who follow a politically correct view of the world. And there is ample evidence here to ascribe Luther with similar egocentric characteristics.

With this mind it is revealing to consider the view of Lawrence Kohlberg, a much-respected psychologist and expert in the study of moral development, who wrote:

"Moral development consists of the growth of less egocentric and more impartial modes of reasoning on more complicated matters."

NO SACRED OXEN

After much soul-searching and many mistakes my advice for anyone intent of beginning an adventure in this world would be to never despair. Despair is a prayer to a dark power but faith is the antidote. There are some relatively recent examples such as the well-documented lives of, Lech Walesa and Aleksandr Solzhenitsyn, who through writing or direct action successfully opposed the yoke of Communism, which had previously crushed entire nations such as Hungary, and later, Czechoslovakia. Who could doubt that without their faith, Solzhenitsyn and Walesa would have found the strength to successfully fight against a dictatorial Communist regime.

Returning again to the protagonist, Martin Luther, it is chilling to find that his rabid anti-Catholic views found such wide appeal in an age as happy and comfortable in its traditions as is revealed earlier by the insight into the English medieval world provided by, Eamon Duffy.

Luther's vitriol is said to have *fanned the flames of nationalism* and that this led to the disintegration of moral and social life of households throughout the Reformation especially in his immediate locality where he sounds utterly hopeless and helpless:

"We live in Sodom and Babylon, affairs are growing daily worse."

Is this a lament for a Catholic Christian world he had ironically played more than an instrumental part in removing from the everyday life of most people in medieval Northern Europe?

Winston Churchill wrote in his autobiography that when faced with his most vulnerable and dangerous moments in South Africa he - unlike Luther - did not bargain with God, but said prayers with the utmost conviction to a *High Power* and attributed this, above all else, to his subsequent outstanding success in life.

Winston also said, *never give in* but sometimes it is wise to beat a hasty retreat and not everyone has the same resolve as an inspired world leader. Perhaps it would be more accurate, if not helpful, to say, *never despair.*

Creativity and healing are more powerful than destruction in the moral hierarchy. Previous to this insight found in Milton's, *Paradise Lost* I had wondered whether destruction was more powerful?

Like many others before and since I had noticed that prolonged effort was often an integral part in achieving anything of worth. It takes time to create something and only seconds to destroy it.

After reading Milton, however, I became aware of the moral superiority of creation and creativity over and above destruction and this view is made explicit in this passage of his magisterial poetry:

> *Before thee; greater now in thy return*
> *Than from the giant angels; thee that day*
> *Thy thunders magnified; but to create*
> *Is greater than created to destroy.*

(Milton, Paradise Lost, Book VII, 604-607).

It is not that Rebellion is inherently bad. Rebellion might sometimes be necessary. It all depends on what you are rebelling against and what is expected to replace it. From the evidence provided it seems that most people within the vicinity of Luther's invective were in a worse state after rebellion than before it.

Indeed, in a few closely connected excerpts from the *Catholic Encyclopedia* on, Martin Luther, it is revealed that what lay beneath religious concerns were:

"... a foundation which was but the consequence of Luther's well-known politics... where freedom of religion became the monopoly of the ruling princes... and, in Germany... serfdom lingered on far longer than any other country save Russia."

Medieval England was secure in its faith but those in power and authority took this faith away from the people and replaced it with something they could control. Today most British political leaders want Britain to be part of the EU and although this means an increasing loss of national sovereignty it is, they say, a price worth paying.

For medieval Man religious change was politicized. For modern Man it is the reverse. Political change has been evangelized using an atheistic creed known as *human rights* and the dogma of *political correctness* to enforce compliance with an ideological orthodoxy intolerant of traditional forms of Western cultural opinion.

Politics has hijacked religion, its creeds, its dogmas and many of its beliefs except those that refer directly to the existence of God, and then subsequently re-written them for a secularized *common purpose* of Cultural Marxism. When there is nothing left to mine, a man-made ideology is implemented as if it were a transcendent religion. In this way political ideology seeps into individual consciousness seeking to rule hearts and minds. The result is an England where people must now think very carefully before voicing an opinion lest someone find their views offensive and contrary to the prevailing political orthodoxy.

A political elite has alienated those holding traditional views of cultural identity by enforcing a politically correct agenda and in so doing deepening feelings of moral superiority and fostering intolerance of those who do not conform. This is not the England I once knew. How have they got away with it? Ultimately it may all depend on whether you prefer rule originating from politicians or priests, from Rome or Brussels? All things considered, I prefer Rome.

Glossary of terms

Atheism: A denial of the existence of God.

Cultural Marxism: A highly influential system of thought arising from Marxian theorists such as Antonio Gramsci (1891-1937) who sought to undermine traditional forms of Western cultural identity.

Determinism: Converse of free will. Doctrine that all things, including will, are determined by causes.

French Revolution: A largely atheistic (the Deist, Voltaire was a notable exception) reformist cultural movement of French intellectuals in the late 18th century, challenging ideas grounded in tradition and faith by emphasizing the pre-eminence of Reason and knowledge gained through the scientific method.

EU: An unaccountable anti-democratic union of nation states (some states are more equal than others) designed with supranational interests in mind although this was never revealed to the population at large. Many ex-communists govern from the heart of this organization.

Free Will: Freedom of choice. Self-determination.

Human Rights Act: A secularist bible.

Humanist: Usually applied in this book as the modern form of humanism espousing, more or less, ideas based upon scientism and atheism.

Left-wing: A broad term identifying those who look to the *Mother State* for solutions to political and social problems.

NO SACRED OXEN

Lucifer: The name of an angel in heaven prior to his rebellion and thereafter named as Satan or the Devil.

Marxism: Political and economic philosophy of Karl Marx and Friedrich Engels in which the concept of class struggle plays a central role in understanding society's allegedly inevitable development from bourgeois oppression under capitalism to a socialist and ultimately classless society. (i)

Paradise Lost: An epic poem written by John Milton in the 17th century about the story of The Fall and eviction of Adam and Eve from the Garden of Eden as first recorded in Genesis in the Christian Bible.

Political Correctness: Adhering to a typically progressive orthodoxy on issues involving especially race, gender, sexual affinity or ecology. (ii)

Predestination: Doctrine that whatever happens has been unalterably fixed by God from the beginning of time.

Reformation: Early 16th century Protestant rebellion against Papal supremacy and Catholicism.

Scientism: Belief that the methods used in studying natural sciences should be employed also in investigating all aspects of human behaviour and condition. (iii)

Schism: A break in the unity of the Church.

Secularism: The belief that the state, morals, education etc, should be independent of religion. (iv)

Sin: A transgression of a religious or moral law, especially when deliberate. (v)

Socialism: Left-wing economic ideology.

Subjectivism: Any view in which the truth of the statement depends on the mental state or reactions of the individual making it. (vi)

Tree of knowledge (of Good and Evil): Many interpret the biblical story of *The Garden of Eden (*where Eve is tempted to eat forbidden fruit from the Tree of Knowledge*)* as an allegory - that is, a story of a terrestrial paradise which has a second meaning beneath the surface.

Trespasses: Sin

Sources:

(i)   Free Dictionary.Com

(ii)   Dictionary.com

(iii)   Chambers Dictionary

(iv)   Chambers Dictionary

(v)   Free Dictionary.com

(vi)   Chambers Dictionary

Afterword

I suppose there are many reasons for my becoming a Catholic and not all of them are easy to explain.

Perhaps it would be easier to say why I found a leap of Christian faith a difficult prospect. It was because I did not think I could live a life that was perfect and spotless. It was not that my behaviour at that time was any better or worse than that of most people but the pressure of having to be a saint was not something I wanted to be burdened with. How many times do the newspapers seek to undermine a man of faith for the glee of shouting, hypocrite! I never wanted that. So my doing a theology degree was more intellectual curiosity than anything else. Nevertheless the time spent learning about my cultural identity has enabled me to understand what a precious heritage we have in the West and that much of our values and beliefs are inherited from a Christian context. For a long time this was the main if only benefit from three years of theological study. But the ensuing thought of not becoming a Christian because of what people might say when I failed began to grate against my conscience. Eventually, some while after an epiphany in Pamplona, I later took that leap and inevitably fell. Fortunately, however, I was not a priest in which case the only real casualty was my own conscience. But I wanted to overcome a life that had spiralled out of control and walking the Camino across Spain was the first step on a very long path. I had accepted that I might fail as a Christian but did not think failure should be a barrier to salvation for a contrite heart seeking forgiveness. I therefore resolved that this would be an arduous journey but in the end successful and that made it necessary for the salvation of my soul as I saw and see it.

Incidentally, Catholic or Christian, these words mean the same thing as far as I am concerned.

Epilogue: A night out in Oxford

It was during the winter of 1992/93 that I stumbled out of the Oxford Union after a night out with some friends from college. I had had a skinful in the downstairs cellar bar imbibing cocktails. Three *Long Island Iced Teas* – several generous shots of gin, vodka, and tequila with coke and ice -and about five pints of cider in the upstairs bar beforehand, was all the Dutch courage I needed when on the way home I became aware of an altercation between *town and gown*.

It was low midnight as the two traditional foes stood facing each other squaring up for a fight. An enthusiastic crowd had gathered. Both pugilists represented their tribe vividly and stereotypically. The tall blond one wore a type of black cape over a white shirt and black trousers. Those supporting him were dressed likewise. The slightly shorter but stockier adversary - I subsequently learnt that he worked in a nearby restaurant - stood his ground and looked like he had a good chin. People were milling about somewhat amused at the evening spectacle before them on this busy Friday night in Oxford.

I was feeling quite pleased with myself as I was wont to do after a night out at the Union and having noticed this confrontation decided to do my good deed for the evening. I wandered over to the middle of the street pushing in between the by now eager participants who were just about to punch each other, when I separated them, saying:

"Alright lads, time to go home now."

Being at least a dozen or so years older, and more than slightly drunk, I had assumed that authority was on my side. I soon found out, however, that this was not the case. No sooner had I walked across back to the pavement than a headbutt hit me full in the face. I could not believe it. I lifted my hand to my mouth to remind me of my new condition, a fat lip.

The culprit was the townie. By now he was walking away. I saw myself as a *good samaritan* and felt aggrieved. So as my assailant was about to be pushed by his friend into a nearby parked-car I punched him several times.

It was *town versus gown* again except this time the gown was represented by someone who had more town background than gown. So there we stood facing each other each waiting for the other to make the next move. The original gown chap had taken my side and stood supporting me. For this I was grateful but not overjoyed at the turn of events, when out of the shadows, a couple of lads ran up the street and waded into me. I hit the deck and ended up horizontal and on the pavement. The gown lad picked me up with comforting words of encouragement. It was by now my second fight of the evening in the space of ten minutes.

The absurdity of it all was not lost on my original townie opponent who had by now left the scene. I got up, dusted myself down and continued on my long walk back home. Things did not go according to plan but it was an eventful and memorable evening. It would be sometime later that I found out that the football fixture for Saturday was Oxford United FC versus Millwall FC. That might explain a few things.

Lightning Source UK Ltd.
Milton Keynes UK
UKOW04f0009250214

227062UK00001B/25/P

9 781909 421417